Cover to Cover 1

Reading Comprehension and Fluency

Richard R. Day and Junko Yamanaka

UNIVERSITY PRESS

Contents

Introduction

Cover to Cover 1 is the first in a three-level reading series that helps students become skilled, strategic readers who enjoy reading in English. *Cover to Cover* combines **intensive reading** with **extensive reading**, so your students will learn the strategies necessary for academic work *and* become fluent, confident readers.

What is intensive reading?

Intensive reading focuses on building language awareness and comprehension. It often involves relatively challenging texts and students encountering some unfamiliar language. Parts 1 and 2 of each unit in *Cover to Cover* focus on intensive reading and provide students with strategies for dealing with these kinds of texts.

What is extensive reading?

Extensive reading focuses on fluency development and reading for pleasure. Two key principles are (1) students should read as much as possible, and (2) texts should be easy and well within students' linguistic competence. Easy texts mean that students are able to read more and faster, and this kind of practice helps students in many ways: improved reading skills, improved writing skills, increased vocabulary knowledge, and increased motivation. The Extensive Reading section at the end of each unit in *Cover to Cover* provides students with an opportunity to experience this approach.

What is in a unit?

Part 1 and **Part 2** of each unit develop reading strategies such as predicting the topic, skimming for the main idea, scanning, and recognizing points of view. Part 1 focuses mainly on comprehension strategies; Part 2 focuses on developing both fluency and comprehension through activities such as timed reading. The reading passages come from a variety of genres including magazine articles, newspaper articles, and web sites.

The **Extensive Reading** section enables students to read for enjoyment and pleasure and continue their fluency development. The reading passages are extracts from the Oxford Bookworms Library collection of graded readers. *Cover to Cover 1* features extracts from stage 1 Bookworms, including popular classics such as *The Phantom of the Opera* and *The Adventures of Tom Sawyer*. The Bookworms extracts are longer than the Part 1 and 2 reading texts, and the language is also graded at a lower level. This enables students to read faster and maintain comprehension. We hope that reading the Bookworms extracts will also motivate students to become enthusiastic, independent readers who read books from cover to cover.

Unit 1

Marriage

Discuss the questions.

1. What is happening in this photograph?
2. When did you last go to a wedding?

This unit is about marriage. In Part 1, you will read about changing views of marriage. In Part 2, you will read about a couple that loves weddings. The unit is followed by Extensive Reading 1, which is an extract from a book called *The Withered Arm*. It is about a woman who is unhappy because the man she loves has just married another woman.

Part 1   To Marry or Not to Marry?

Before Reading

Discuss the questions.

1. At what age do women get married in your country?

2. At what age do men get married?

Comprehension Strategy: Finding Main Ideas in Paragraphs

Every paragraph has a main idea. This is the most important thing the writer wants to say. The main idea is often near the beginning of the paragraph.

A. **Read the text. Write the paragraph number next to its main idea.**

  _2_ **a.** A growing number of Japanese women are happy to be single.

  ...... **b.** In Japan, attitudes toward marriage are changing.

  ...... **c.** Many working women do not want to be traditional wives.

  ...... **d.** These days, women are looking for different kinds of husbands.

  ...... **e.** The number of single women in their 20s has increased.

  ...... **f.** Sumi Kitade is happy to be single.

B. **Read the text again and answer the questions that follow.**

🎧 *CD 1 Track 2*

To Marry or Not to Marry?

1   Attitudes toward marriage are changing in Japan. In the past, most women were expected to be married by the time they were 25. Women who were not married by then were often thought to have missed out. These single women were sometimes even compared to Christmas cake on December 26th–old and not wanted. Now, things are very different.

2   According to an opinion poll in a Japanese newspaper, *The Daily Yomiuri,* 73 percent of single Japanese women say they are happy to be single. This is an increase of 10 percent since 2003.

3   Dr. Sumi Kitade is one of them. She laughs and smiles as she discusses her future. "I will continue my career as a professor," Dr. Kitade says. "I love my

work. It's very exciting." When asked about getting married, the 30-year-old professor becomes serious. "To tell the truth," she replies, "I don't think I will ever get married. I am happy. I have a wonderful job and I have many friends."

4   This attitude is reflected in the increase in the number of single women. In 1970, 18 percent of Japanese women between the ages of 25 and 29 were not married. Thirty years later, that figure had risen to well over 50 percent.

5   The reasons can be found in the workplace and at home. On the one hand, more women have full-time jobs than 30 years ago. On the other hand, the traditional role of the wife has not changed. Women are still expected to raise the children and look after the house. They often don't get much help from their husbands. Many women manage the house in addition to doing a full-time job. One survey found that working women spend two hours each day on housework, while men spend about ten minutes. Young working women may choose not to take on these extra responsibilities. Sumi Kitade appears to support this view. "I don't want to quit my job to become someone's slave," says Dr. Kitade.

Sumi Kitade

6   In the past, women looked for husbands who could offer financial support. Now, women are looking for something different. Kaoru Abe, one of Dr. Kitade's colleagues, is 34. She is looking for a husband who will look after the children and share the housework equally. She says she has nothing against marriage. She just hasn't found the right man yet. If her ideal man is out there, she will be very happy. And if he isn't, she says, she'll be happy on her own.

Checking Comprehension

Answer the questions.

1. What is the main idea of this article?
   a. A growing number of Japanese women are happy to be single.
   b. Sumi Kitade is happy to be single.
   c. Men don't do as much housework as women.

2. Why did single women over the age of 25 used to be compared to Christmas cake?
   a. People thought they were happy to be single.
   b. People thought they were too old to get married.
   c. People thought they ate too much.

3. Why doesn't Sumi Kitade want to get married?
   a. She can't find her ideal man.
   b. She is too busy working to look for a husband.
   c. She is happy to be single.

4. Which of the following is true of Kaoru Abe?
   a. She is looking for a traditional husband.
   b. She does not want to get married.
   c. She is looking for a husband who will share the housework.

5. What did the opinion poll show?
   a. 73 percent of women in Japan are single.
   b. 73 percent of women in Japan are happy.
   c. 73 percent of single women in Japan are happy to be single.

6. What is one reason that there are more single women now than in 1970?
   a. Men don't do as much housework as they did in 1970.
   b. More women have full-time jobs than in 1970.
   c. Fewer men can provide financial support than in 1970.

Looking at Vocabulary in Context

A. Find the words in bold in the text. For each line, circle the word that does not belong.

1. **attitudes** (par. 1)	viewpoints	outlooks	heights
2. **increase** (par. 2)	growth	decrease	rise
3. **continue** (par. 3)	go on with	keep on	stop
4. **traditional** (par. 5)	old-fashioned	conservative	modern
5. **responsibilities** (par. 5)	answers	duties	tasks
6. **quit** (par. 5)	keep on	stop	leave

B. Fill in the blanks with the words in bold from A. Be sure to use the correct forms.

1. The soccer coach was so mean that three players ....

2. Airfares are getting more expensive because of the .... in fuel prices.

3. Lisa has a very bad .... at work. She's so lazy.

4. I am always busy in my new job because I have so many different ....

5. I hate using microwave ovens. I prefer cooking on the stove the .... way.

6. You must .... your diet if you want to lose more weight.

What's Your Opinion?

A. Do you agree or disagree with the statements? Check (✔) your answers.

	Agree	Disagree	Not Sure
1. There are more advantages to being single than being married.	☐	☐	☐
2. It is better to get married when you are young.	☐	☐	☐
3. People can be happy if they never get married.	☐	☐	☐
4. People should not get married unless they find their ideal partner.	☐	☐	☐
5. Men should do more housework.	☐	☐	☐

B. Discuss your answers with a partner. Give reasons for your answers.

Before Reading

Discuss the questions.

1. What is the relationship between the people in the photo?
2. How long do you think they have known each other?

Fluency Strategy: Scanning

Scanning is searching very fast for specific information—a fact, a number, a word, a phrase. Make a clear picture in your mind of the information you are looking for. Move your eyes quickly across the text. Don't read every word. When you find the information, stop and read the sentence.

A. **Scan the text for the numbers. Match them with the information.**

....	**a.** 4	1. Antonio's age when he first saw Maria.
....	**b.** 19	2. The date in July when Maria and Antonio were married.
....	**c.** 17	3. Maria's age when she married Antonio.
....	**d.** 18	4. Maria's age when she first saw Antonio.

B. **Read the whole text quickly. Record your reading time below and on the chart on page 169.**

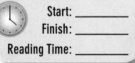

Start: _____
Finish: _____
Reading Time: _____

🎧 *CD 1 Track 3*

The Couple That Loves Weddings

1   It is a happy wedding day. The bride and groom are congratulated by their friends and relatives. Everyone is having a wonderful time at the wedding party.

2   But this is not the first time that Maria Foti has celebrated her wedding. In fact, it is her thirtieth wedding party. But she has married the same man each time. The couple told their story to *Reflections* magazine.

3   Antonio Foti was 19 years old when he first saw Maria Santos. He was working at his father's store. Antonio smiles as he remembers that day. "Maria came into the store to buy some food," he says. Maria was unable to find what she wanted, so she asked Antonio. "I could only stare at her," says Antonio.

Antonio and Maria

"I thought Maria was the most beautiful girl in the world." He promised himself that he would marry her.

4   Unfortunately for Antonio, Maria was just a young girl, only 17 years old. She was still in high school. But Antonio did not want to wait. He asked his father to talk to Maria's father, Mr. Santos. Antonio's father thought his son was too young to get married. But Antonio kept asking, so Mr. Foti went to talk to Maria's father.

5   Mr. Foti told Mr. Santos that his son wanted to marry Maria. Both fathers thought that Maria was too young. Mr. Santos wanted them to wait one year, until Maria was 18, and she had finished high school.

6   Antonio was unhappy with the decision. He was impatient, but he had no choice. "That one year seemed like ten years for me," he says. When Maria finished high school, her father told her that she could marry Antonio. Maria and Antonio were married on July 4, 1954.

7   Neither family had a lot of money, so they had a small wedding ceremony. After the wedding, there was a small party at a restaurant. Everyone had a lot of fun eating, dancing, and singing.

8   Maria and Antonio were very happy. After one year of marriage, they wanted to have another wedding. They asked the priest who had married them if it was possible to do it again. And they had another party at the same restaurant. Like the first time, everyone had fun.

9   Now, every July 4, they have another wedding and a party for their relatives and friends at the usual restaurant. Unlike the first wedding and party, many people attend, including Maria and Antonio's children and grandchildren.

Checking Fluency and Comprehension

A. **Answer the questions. Do not look back at the text.**

1. What was Antonio doing when he first saw Maria?
   a. Studying at high school.
   b. Buying food.
   c. Working in a store.

2. What did Maria's father think?
   a. He thought they should wait to get married until Antonio was 18.
   b. He thought they should wait to get married until Maria was 18.
   c. He thought they should wait to get married until Maria was 19.

3. Why was their first wedding small?
   a. They did not have space for many people.
   b. They did not have a lot of money.
   c. Their families did not want them to get married.

4. Where do they have the party every year?
   a. At the same restaurant as their first wedding.
   b. At a bigger restaurant.
   c. At their house.

5. How long did Antonio have to wait before he married Maria?
   a. One year.
   b. Two years.
   c. 10 years.

B. **Check your answers with a partner. Record your score on page 169.**

Expanding Vocabulary

A. **Antonyms are words with the opposite meaning. Find the antonyms of these words in the text.**

1. able (par.3) ....
2. happy (par.6) ....
3. patient (par.6) ....

4. impossible (par.8) ....
5. unusual (par.9) ....
6. like (par.9) ....

B. Fill in the blanks with the words from A.

1. I only like movies with .... endings—I hate sad ones.

2. The final test question was ...., so everyone just guessed.

3. My computer has a virus so I've been .... to send email.

4. So many pop stars sound .... all the others—it's boring.

5. Drivers who always honk their horns are just being ....

6. I have a very .... name—no one has ever heard it before.

What's Your Opinion?

A. **What do you think makes a good marriage? Check (✔) your answers.**

	Important	Not Important
1. Approval of couple's parents	☐	☐
2. A big wedding	☐	☐
3. A lot of money	☐	☐
4. One child	☐	☐
5. Many children	☐	☐

B. **Discuss your answers with a partner. Give reasons for your answers.**

Increasing Fluency

Scan the line to find the word on the left. Words may appear more than once. Can you finish in 15 seconds?

	a	b	c	d	e
1. marry	merry	marry	many	marry	married
2. father	rather	further	farther	father	father
3. party	party	pretty	part	partner	parties
4. fun	run	bun	gun	nun	fun
5. year	near	year	year	dear	fear
6. wait	weight	wait	waits	weigh	wait
7. young	you	young	youth	hung	young
8. only	lonely	any	only	only	oily

Extensive Reading 1

The Withered Arm

Introduction

This extract from an Oxford *Bookworms* reader gives you the opportunity to read more in English. The more you read, the faster and more fluent you will become. *The Withered Arm* is set on a farm in England in the 19th century. The farm is owned by Mr. Lodge. He has a new wife, named Gertrude, who is young and pretty. Mr. Lodge's first love, Rhoda Brook, lives nearby with their son. The extract you will read starts a few weeks after Gertrude Lodge comes to live on the farm. Rhoda hasn't met Gertrude, but she feels jealous, and she can't stop thinking about her. She even dreams about her. But is it more than just a dream?

Before Reading

A. **What do you think will happen in the extract? Check (✔) your answers.**

.... **1.** Rhoda dreams that Gertrude is friendly and kind.

.... **2.** Rhoda dreams that Gertrude is cruel and unfriendly.

.... **3.** Rhoda dreams that Gertrude leaves the farm.

.... **4.** Rhoda dreams that she hurts Gertrude's arm.

B. **Now read the extract to see what happens.**

🎧 *CD 1 Track 4*

Words

Rhoda Brook sat by the dying fire in her little house. She stared at the fire for a long time, but she saw only the picture in her head of the new wife. At last, tired from her day's work, she went to bed.

But the picture of Gertrude Lodge did not go away. When Rhoda slept, the young wife was still there in Rhoda's dreams. She sat on Rhoda's body in the bed, staring into Rhoda's face. Her blue eyes were cold, and with a cruel laugh, she put her left hand in front of Rhoda's eyes. There, on the third finger, was her wedding ring. And the phantom of Gertrude Lodge laughed again.

50

100

Rhoda turned this way and that way, but the phantom was still there. It sat, heavier and heavier, on Rhoda's body, and now Rhoda could not move. Always in her ears was that cruel laugh, and always in front of her eyes was that left hand with its wedding ring.

At last, half-dead with terror, Rhoda suddenly put out her right hand, took hold of the phantom's left arm, and pulled it hard.

The phantom fell off the bed onto the floor, and Rhoda sat up.

"Dear God!" she cried. She felt cold, so cold. "That was not a dream—she was here!"

She could still feel the young woman's arm under her hand—a warm, living arm. She looked on the floor for the woman's body, but there was nothing there.

Rhoda Brook slept no more that night, and at the dairy early the next morning, she looked pale and sick. She could not forget the feel of that arm under her hand.

When she came home for breakfast, her son asked her, "What was that noise in your room last night, mother? Did you fall off the bed?"

"Noise? What time did you hear it?"

"About two o'clock. But what was it, mother? Something fell, I heard it. Was it you?"

Rhoda did not answer, and after breakfast she began to do her work in the house. At about midday she heard something, and looked out of the window. At the bottom of the garden stood a woman—the woman from her dream. Rhoda stood still, and stared.

* * *

Rhoda's son tells her that he met Gertrude Lodge on the road. Mrs. Lodge felt sorry for him because he was wearing old shoes so she said she would buy him some new shoes. Mrs. Lodge brings the shoes to the house and is very kind and polite. Rhoda is surprised and starts to think of her as more of a friend than an enemy.

* * *

Two days later Mrs. Lodge came again, with a new shirt for the boy, and twelve days after that she visited Rhoda a third time. The boy was out that day.

"I like walking up here on the hill," Mrs. Lodge told Rhoda. "And your house is the only one up here."

They talked about the weather and the village, then

250

300

350

400

450

500

Mrs. Lodge got up to leave. "Are you well, Rhoda?" she asked. 'You look pale."

"Oh, I'm always pale," said Rhoda. "But what about you, Mrs. Lodge? Are you well?"

"Yes, I am, but...there is something...It's nothing very bad, but I don't understand it."

She uncovered her left hand and arm. There were marks on the arm, yellowy-brown marks, like marks made by fingers. Rhoda stared at them.

"How did it happen?" she asked.

"I don't know," said Mrs. Lodge. "One night, when I was in bed, I had a dream...and then suddenly, my arm hurt very badly. Perhaps I hit it on something in the daytime, but I don't remember it." She laughed. "My dear husband says it's nothing very much, and he's right, of course."

"Yes...Which night was that?" said Rhoda.

Mrs. Lodge thought for a moment. "It was two weeks ago today. It was two o'clock in the night—I remember, because I heard the clock."

It was the same night, the same hour, as Rhoda's dream of the phantom. Rhoda remembered the terror of it, and felt cold.

"How can this be?" she thought, when Mrs. Lodge left. "Did I do that? But why? She is innocent and kind—I don't want to hurt her. And how can a thing like that happen? Only witches can do things like that..."

Extract from *The Withered Arm*, Bookworms Readers, Oxford University Press.

After Reading

Answer the questions.

1. What did Rhoda do to the phantom in her dream?

   ....

2. What did Rhoda's son hear?

   ....

3. What did Mrs. Lodge bring Rhoda's son?

   ....

4. What was wrong with Mrs. Lodge's left arm?

   ....

Thinking About the Story

Answer the questions.

1. Did you enjoy reading the extract? Do you want to read more about Rhoda and Mrs. Lodge?
2. Do you think Rhoda is a witch?
3. What do you think will happen to Mrs. Lodge's arm?

Timed Repeated Reading

How many words can you read in one minute? Follow the instructions to practice increasing your reading speed.

1. Time yourself. Read the extract for one minute. When you stop, underline the last word you read and write 'first' in the margin.
2. Go back to the beginning of the extract. Read again for one minute. Try to read faster this time. When you stop, underline the last word you read and write 'second' in the margin.
3. Go back to the beginning of the extract. Read again for one minute. Try to read even faster this time. When you stop, underline the last word you read and write 'third' in the margin.
4. Count the number of words you read each time. Record the three numbers on the Timed Repeated Reading Chart on page 169.

Unit 2

Reading Strategies
- Comprehension: Identifying Meaning from Context
- Fluency: Skimming for the Main Idea

Sleep

Discuss the questions.

1. How much sleep do you think most people need?
2. Do you think you get enough sleep?

This unit is about sleep. In Part 1, you will read about how much sleep people need. In Part 2, you will read about a university student's sleeping habits. The unit is followed by Extensive Reading 2, which is an extract from a book called *The President's Murderer*. It is about a man who is afraid to sleep, because he is being chased by police.

Getting Enough Sleep

Before Reading

Discuss the questions.

1. Do teenagers need more sleep than other people?

2. Have you ever fallen asleep in a public place?

Comprehension Strategy: Identifying Meaning from Context

You can often work out the meaning of words you don't know from the words and phrases nearby. Try to work out the part of speech (noun, verb, adjective, adverb) of the new word. Look at the sentences before and after the word. They may use words with the same meaning, or with the opposite meaning.

A. **Find the words in bold in the text. Use the strategy to work out the meanings, then circle the answers.**

1. **Nodded off** (par. 1) probably has *a similar / the opposite* meaning to "stay awake."

2. **Sleep deprivation** (par. 4) probably has *a similar / the opposite* meaning to "not getting the amount of sleep someone needs."

3. **Impaired** (par. 6) probably has *a similar / the opposite* meaning to "badly affected."

B. **Read the text again and answer the questions that follow.**

CD 1 Track 5

Getting Enough Sleep

1   The lecture hall is filled with about 60 students, all around 18 or 19 years old. The professor is explaining a point about economic theory to the class. It is nine o'clock in the morning, but some of the students seem to be finding it hard to stay awake. A few have nodded off completely. It could be that they are bored with the lecture. But, according to researchers, it is more likely that they simply haven't had enough sleep.

2   Experts say that most teenagers need about nine hours of sleep a night. This is more than either adults or children need. For most adults, seven to eight hours a night is generally enough, although the exact amount is different for each person. Infants, who need about 16 hours a day, are the only age group that needs more sleep than teenagers.

3   However, research shows that many teenagers are not getting the amount of sleep they need. In one survey, around half the teenagers interviewed said they slept an average of six hours a night. That is three hours less than experts say they should get.

4   Teenagers aren't the only ones who aren't getting enough sleep. In many societies, sleep deprivation is becoming part of the culture. When people "work hard and play hard," there is not much time left for sleep. These people often see the symptoms of sleep deprivation as part of normal life. For example, a person might think he or she is yawning because of boredom. In fact, experts say it means they probably haven't had enough sleep.

5   The problem can get worse over time. When people have too little sleep over a long period, they build up a "sleep debt." If a person misses one hour of sleep every night for a week, then by the end of the week he or she will need to catch up on seven hours of sleep.

6   The effects of sleep deprivation can be serious. Research shows that people who don't get enough sleep find it hard to make decisions. Their work or studies can be badly affected. Their ability to drive can also be impaired. Thousands of traffic accidents each year are caused by sleep deprived people. In addition, long-term sleep disorders can cause high blood pressure and may lead to heart attacks.

7   Drinking coffee, or soft drinks with caffeine, cannot help people who are sleep deprived. There is only one thing to do if you feel sleepy: start going to bed earlier.

Checking Comprehension

A. These sentences are false. Complete the new sentences with correct information.

1. Adults need the same amount of sleep as teenagers.

   Adults need ....

2. Teenagers should probably sleep about six hours every night.

   Teenagers should probably sleep about ....

3. Infants need less sleep than adults.

   Infants need ....

4. People yawn when they are bored.

   People yawn when ....

5. Drivers with sleeping problems cause a few traffic accidents each year.

   Drivers with sleeping problems cause ....

6. Coffee helps people who have sleep problems.

   Coffee ....

B. Fill in the blanks with these words.

sixteen	impair	cause	caffeine	seven	nod off

Every day, adults should get at least (1) .... hours of sleep,

while infants need around (2) .... hours of sleep. Sleep

disorders can (3) .... serious problems. Not sleeping

enough can (4) .... your ability to make decisions. People

who (5) .... while they are driving might have a traffic

accident. (6) .... cannot solve sleep problems.

Looking at Vocabulary in Context

A. Find the words in bold in the text. Circle the correct definitions.

1. **Experts** (par. 2) are people *with special knowledge or skills / who are not paid for their work.*

2. If you sleep for an **average** (par. 3) of six hours a night, you sleep *for exactly six hours every night / more on some nights and less other nights.*

3. **Deprivation** (par. 4) means *having enough of something / not having enough of something.*

4. **Symptoms** (par. 4) of an illness are the *signs / causes* of the illness.

5. A **debt** (par. 5) is *something you must pay back / a special advantage.*

6. **Disorders** (par. 6) are *illnesses / accidents.*

B. Fill in the blanks with the words in bold from A. Be sure to use the correct forms.

1. Sandy took out many loans for medical school, so it will take him a long time to pay off his _____.

2. I want the advice of an _____, so I hired the best lawyer in town.

3. The _____ temperature in San Francisco during the summer is 17 degrees.

4. That medical practice takes care of people with eating _____.

5. Food _____ is a big problem in many African countries.

6. Common _____ of the flu include fever, sore throat, and pain.

What's Your Opinion?

A. Do you agree or disagree with the statements? Check (✔) your answers.

	Agree	Disagree	Not Sure
1. It's OK to sleep in class if you're tired.	☐	☐	☐
2. I can make good decisions even when I'm tired.	☐	☐	☐
3. I sleep longer hours on the weekend.	☐	☐	☐
4. I often drink caffeine to help me stay awake.	☐	☐	☐
5. People who are tired shouldn't be allowed to drive.	☐	☐	☐

B. Discuss your answers with a partner.

Before Reading

Discuss the questions.

1. What is your usual daily routine?
2. Do you sleep more or less than other people your age?

Fluency Strategy: Skimming for the Main Idea

Skimming is reading fast to understand the writer's main idea, or message. Read the title, the first paragraph, and the first sentences in the other paragraphs. Then read the last paragraph. Read quickly; details are not important.

A. **Use the strategy to skim the text. Circle the main idea.**

1. Experts think my sleep habits are unhealthy.
2. Some world leaders have been famous for not sleeping much.
3. Don't listen to expert advice about sleeping if you want to be successful.

B. **Read the whole text quickly. Record your reading time below and on the chart on page 169.**

Start: _____
Finish: _____
Reading Time: _____

🎧 *CD 1 Track 6*

The Experts Are Wrong!
Posted by: Young-soo Kim, August 4th

1   I am a 17-year-old high school student in Seoul, Korea. I also work part-time at a store that my parents own, so I am very busy. I only have time to sleep three or four hours each night.

2   I know this is less than experts say we need, but I don't plan to change. I think a lot of expert advice is unrealistic. If you slept the number of hours that they recommend, you would spend a third of your life sleeping. If I slept that much, I would never have time to do all the things I do now.

3   During the week, my day begins at six o'clock. From seven in the morning to seven in the evening, I go to school and attend classes, participate in club activities, and study. From seven to nine in the evening, I go to a private school

called a *hagwon* to study for university entrance exams. At ten o'clock, I go to my parents' store and work until two in the morning. I go to sleep from about two-thirty until my day starts again at six o'clock. On the weekend, I work longer hours at the store, and I usually get to sleep in until eight.

4   Experts might think that my sleeping habits aren't healthy. Some might even say I have a sleep disorder, but I don't think I have a problem. I feel very healthy and full of energy. I am never sick. Well, I'm almost never sick. Sometimes I have colds, but I take vitamins to get over them quickly. I exercise nearly every day. I also play soccer at school, and I go to a gym on the weekend.

5   I think you have to push yourself to be really successful. I want to get a good job and earn a lot of money, so I need to work hard and get into a good university. I can afford to have less sleep now if it means I'll have a better chance in a future job interview. World leaders like John F. Kennedy and Margaret Thatcher were famous for not sleeping much. If it worked for the President of the United States and the Prime Minister of Britain, then it can't be such a bad idea.

6   Here is my advice: if you want to be successful, then don't listen to the experts. Some of them don't understand what it takes to get ahead.

Checking Fluency and Comprehension

A. **Complete the sentences. Do not look back at the text.**

1. Young-soo studies at a *hagwon* ....
   a. from seven in the morning to seven in the evening.
   b. in the morning, from two-thirty to six o'clock.
   c. in the evening, from seven o'clock to nine o'clock.

2. After studying at a private school, Young-soo ....
   a. goes to sleep.
   b. works at a part-time job.
   c. plays soccer.

3. On weekends, Young-soo gets up .... on week days.
   a. later than
   b. earlier than
   c. at the same time as

4. Young-soo takes vitamins to ....
   a. get more sleep.
   b. feel better when he's sick.
   c. study and exercise more often.

5. To get ahead in life, Young-soo thinks he should ....
   a. listen to world leaders.
   b. work hard and stay healthy.
   c. sleep less than three hours a night.

B. **Check your answers with a partner. Record your score on page 169.**

Expanding Vocabulary

A. **Find the verbs or adjectives in the text that are related to these nouns.**

1. recommendation (par. 2) .... 4. health (par. 4) ....

2. attendance (par. 3) .... 5. success (par. 5) ....

3. participation (par. 3) .... 6. fame (par. 5) ....

B. Fill in the blanks with the nouns, adjectives, or verbs from A.

1. The doctor says I am very fit and _____.

2. You need to work hard to be _____ in your career.

3. I didn't understand what everyone was talking about, so I couldn't really _____ in their conversation.

4. When Penelope Cruz started starring in Hollywood films, her _____ spread around the world.

5. I chose the restaurant because of a friend's _____.

6. I missed lots of classes last semester, so the college said my _____ must improve this year.

What's Your Opinion?

A. How often do you do these things? Check (✔) your answers.

	Often	Sometimes	Never
1. sleep more than eight hours a night	☐	☐	☐
2. study late at night	☐	☐	☐
3. exercise on the weekend	☐	☐	☐
4. take vitamins	☐	☐	☐
5. get sick	☐	☐	☐

B. Discuss your answers with a partner. Who do you think has better habits?

Increasing Fluency

Scan the line to find the word on the left. Words may appear more than once. Can you finish in 15 seconds?

	a	b	c	d	e
1. hours	ours	hour	hours	sours	fours
2. spend	spend	sped	spent	send	spend
3. colds	cold	colds	scold	sold	holds
4. push	plush	bush	posh	push	rush
5. sleep	sleep	sheep	sleep	sleet	seep
6. nearly	yearly	nearly	nearly	early	pearly
7. stay	stray	stay	stays	slay	clay
8. takes	takes	stake	taker	steak	tales

Extensive Reading 2

The President's Murderer

Introduction

This extract from an Oxford *Bookworms* reader gives you the opportunity to read more in English. The more you read, the faster and more fluent you will become. *The President's Murderer* is about a police hunt for a man named Alex Dinon. He was found guilty of murdering the President. He was put in jail for life, but he escaped. The police almost caught him but he got away. They have been searching for him for the last 24 hours. Both Dinon and the police are very tired. The extract you will read starts with the Chief of Police, Eva Hine, speaking to Felix, a young police inspector.

Before Reading

A. **What do you think will happen in the extract? Check (✔) your answers.**

...... **1.** Dinon falls asleep, and the police catch him.

...... **2.** Dinon falls asleep, and an old lady finds him.

...... **3.** The police inspector falls asleep, and Dinon gets away.

...... **4.** The Chief of Police brings Dinon back to jail.

B. **Now read the extract to see what happens.**

🎧 *CD 1 Track 7*

	Words
"What are you saying? You lost him?" the Chief of Police said angrily.	
The young police inspector in front of her was tired. Very tired. He wanted to sit down, but people did not sit down in the Chief's office. They stood and waited, and perhaps the Chief said, "Sit down." *Then* they sat down— but not before.	50
So the inspector stood. "I'm sorry, Chief," he said. "We couldn't find him in the trees. We looked all night, but it was dark and…"	
The Chief of Police put her hands on the desk in front of her. "You had five men with you, Inspector, and two	100

dogs. And you couldn't find him!"

Eva Hine, the Chief of Police, was a tall woman of about fifty. Her eyes were gray and very cold. Dangerous eyes. When Eva Hine said "Jump!," people jumped. They did not ask questions first.

The inspector waited, and the Chief of Police looked at him coldly. "What are you waiting for?" she asked. "Go out and find him! Three months ago this man— Alex Dinon—killed the President of our country. He's a murderer—a dangerous man. Twenty-four hours ago he escaped from prison, and our new President wants him back in prison—today! Now! At once!"

The inspector quickly left the room.

His name was Felix, and he was thirty-three years old. That was young for an inspector, but he was a good policeman. He liked his job, and worked long hours, but he was sometimes afraid of Eva Hine, the Chief of Police.

Ten minutes later he was back in his office, and Adam came into his room. Adam was twenty-five, and usually worked with Felix on important jobs.

"What did the Chief say?" Adam asked.

"Find Dinon quickly," Felix said. "So, let's begin. Have we got photographs of Dinon? And what about his family?"

Adam put some photographs on the desk. "He's got a wife and two young children," he said.

"Right. I want photographs on television and in all the newspapers. Four men can watch his house and family, day and night—four hours on, and four hours off. Next, I want policemen at all the airports and…"

Telephones rang, and people came and went in the office. Felix and Adam worked on, late into the night.

The next morning Alex Dinon was forty kilometers south of the prison. He moved quickly and stayed away from towns and villages. It was winter and the weather was cold, so there were not many people in the fields. He looked behind him often, but nobody saw him and nobody followed him.

At midday he found a quiet field and lay down under some small trees. He slept at once.

At about three o'clock Alex opened his eyes, and saw an old woman in front of him.

"What are you doing in my field, young man?" she said.

Alex sat up quickly. "I'm sorry," he said. "I was tired, and

450

needed some sleep. I'm going now."

"You're very dirty," the old woman said. "Look at you! Where are you going?"

"North," Alex said. He stood up and began to move away.

"Don't run away. I'm only an old woman." She looked at him carefully. "You're dirty, and hungry, and tired…and afraid. Am I right?"

Alex smiled slowly. "Yes," he said.

"Well, come back to my house and have some food. And you can have some of my husband's old clothes. He died last winter."

Alex looked at her. It was true. He was hungry and tired and dirty. And afraid…but not of this old woman.

"Thank you very much," he said.

The old woman's name was Marta. Her house was very small, but she put some wonderful hot food in front of Alex. He ate quickly, and Marta watched him.

"Oh, you *were* hungry," she laughed.

Alex smiled, but did not stop eating.

Marta found some old clothes for him, and then made some coffee. She said nothing, but watched him with a smile. Alex finished eating and drank some coffee. He began to feel better.

"How did you escape from prison?" Marta asked suddenly.

Alex's face went white. He stared at Marta and said

nothing.

Marta laughed. "It's all right," she said. "I'm not afraid of the President's murderer. You can stay here tonight, Alex Dinon, and have a good sleep. I don't like the police,

and I'm not going to tell them."

Extract from *The President's Murderer,* Bookworms Library, Oxford University Press.

After Reading

Answer the questions.

1. Why is the Chief of Police angry?

   ....

2. What does Felix want to put on television and in newspapers?

   ....

3. Where does Dinon go to sleep?

   ....

4. How does Marta help Dinon?

   ....

Thinking About the Story

Answer the questions.

1. Did you enjoy reading the extract? Do you want to read more about the President's murderer?
2. Why do you think Marta helped Alex Dinon?
3. Do you think the police will catch Alex?

Timed Repeated Reading

How many words can you read in one minute? Follow the instructions to practice increasing your reading speed.

1. Time yourself. Read the extract for one minute. When you stop, underline the last word you read and write "first" in the margin.
2. Go back to the beginning of the extract. Read again for one minute. Try to read faster this time. When you stop, underline the last word you read and write "second" in the margin.
3. Go back to the beginning of the extract. Read again for one minute. Try to read even faster this time. When you stop, underline the last word you read and write "third" in the margin.
4. Count the number of words you read each time. Record the three numbers on the Timed Repeated Reading Chart on page 169.

Unit 3

The Supernatural

Discuss the questions.

1. Have you ever asked someone to tell you what will happen in your future?

2. Are you superstitious? Do you believe in good and bad luck?

This unit is about the supernatural—things that cannot be explained by science. In Part 1, you will read about someone who says they have special abilities. In Part 2, you will read about beliefs around the world. The unit is followed by Extensive Reading 3, which is an extract from a book called *The Phantom of the Opera*. It is about a ghost that people believe lives in an opera house.

Part 1 — An Extra Sense?

Before Reading

Discuss the questions.

1. What is a "sixth sense"?
2. Do some people know what will happen in the future?

Comprehension Strategy: Finding Main Ideas in Paragraphs

> Every paragraph has a main idea. This is the most important thing the writer wants to say. The main idea is often near the beginning of the paragraph.

A. **Read the text. Write the paragraph number with its main idea.**

  1 **a.** Naomi says she has psychic powers.

     b. Psychics will continue to be popular in the future.

     c. Many Americans believe in extrasensory perception.

     d. Skeptics say ESP does not exist.

     e. Carla is a client who believes in Naomi's powers.

     f. The term "ESP" dates back to the 1930s.

B. **Read the text again and answer the questions that follow.**

🎧 *CD 1 Track 8*

An Extra Sense?

1   Naomi says that when the phone rings, she knows who is calling. She knows, that is, before she picks up the phone. She also knows what people are going to say before they say it. Naomi says she is psychic. She says she has a sixth sense, also known as "extrasensory perception," or ESP. Naomi works as a psychic in New York City. She gives people advice about their careers, relationships, and many other areas of their lives. She has had visits from some famous people, but she won't say who.

2   Carla, a 23-year-old shop assistant, is one of Naomi's clients. "She told me so many things about myself that she couldn't have known," says Carla. "She knew I was engaged to be married. She also said I didn't like my job, and she was right both times!" Naomi also advised Carla to take a course in graphic design.

Naomi

Carla was amazed. She had always wanted to do something more creative. Now she has signed up for a design course in college.

3   Carla is not alone. Thousands of people visit psychics, and Americans spend 300 million dollars a year on telephone calls to psychic hotlines. As many as half of all Americans believe in ESP.

4   The term ESP was first used by researchers in the 1930s. They did experiments with a pack of cards. They asked people to predict what was on the cards. The researchers believed people must be using an extra sense to predict some of the cards correctly.

5   However, many people are skeptical about the idea of ESP. They think it does not exist. They say that, first of all, psychics just make good guesses. They use clues, such as a client's age and appearance, to guess things about their lives. Some guesses turn out to be correct, while others do not. However, clients often only remember the correct guesses. They sometimes forget the times when the psychic is wrong. Secondly, psychics often make a lot of very general statements. These statements are true for many people, so they have a good chance of being right. For example, a psychic may tell a client, "You are usually sociable, but you sometimes feel shy." This description is probably true for many people. However, the client may think it is a unique description of himself or herself.

6   Skeptics and believers in ESP can probably agree on one prediction— people will continue to visit psychics like Naomi well into the future.

Checking Comprehension

Answer the questions.

1. What is the main topic of the article?
   - **a.** Extrasensory perception.
   - **b.** Psychics working in New York.
   - **c.** The number of people who visit psychics.

2. What does the author of the article think about ESP?
   - **a.** It exists.
   - **b.** It doesn't exist.
   - **c.** The author doesn't give an opinion.

3. What is true of Carla?
   - **a.** Carla thinks Naomi made a lucky guess.
   - **b.** Carla didn't believe in ESP before visiting Naomi.
   - **c.** Carla believes Naomi has psychic powers.

4. What did Carla do as a result of her visit to Naomi?
   - **a.** She got engaged to be married.
   - **b.** She decided to visit Naomi regularly.
   - **c.** She decided to take a class.

5. Why did researchers first use the term ESP?
   - **a.** To describe an extra sense.
   - **b.** To describe people who were good at guessing.
   - **c.** To describe people who had excellent sight and hearing.

6. What might a skeptic NOT think about Carla's experience?
   - **a.** Carla only remembered the correct things Naomi said.
   - **b.** Naomi used a sixth sense to tell Carla about her life.
   - **c.** Naomi used her five senses to make guesses about Carla.

Looking at Vocabulary in Context

A. **Find the words in bold in the text. Match the definitions.**

...... **1. psychic** (par. 1)   **a.**   say that something will happen in the future

...... **2. clients** (par. 2)   **b.**   able to make new or different things

...... **3. creative** (par. 2)   **c.**   people who receive a service

...... **4. predict** (par. 4)   **d.**   doubtful that something is true

...... **5. skeptical** (par. 5)   **e.**   being the only one; unusual

...... **6. unique** (par. 5)   **f.**   having unusual powers, such as knowing what someone is thinking

B. **Fill in the blanks with the words from A.**

My brother claims to have (1) .... abilities. He says that he

can (2) .... when good or bad luck will happen for someone.

He thinks his powers are (3) ...., but I think a lot of people

say they can do the same thing. I am (4) .... of his statements

because I never believe anything he says. I think he is just lazy and he wants

a lot of (5) .... who will pay him money to hear that they will

be rich and famous in the future. I think it would be better if he spent his

time on a (6) .... hobby like making art or music.

What's Your Opinion?

A. **Interview other people in your class. For each question, find someone who answers "Yes" and write their name.**

	Name
1. Do you believe that you are psychic?	....
2. Do you know someone who has a sixth sense?	....
3. Do you not believe in stories about ESP?	....
4. Do you want to be psychic?	....
5. Have you visited a psychic?	....

B. **Tell the rest of the class what you found out.**

Before Reading

Discuss what you would do in this situation.

You arrive at a hotel. Your room number is an unlucky number. What would you do?

    a. Ask the hotel to change your room.

    b. Stay in the room feeling uncomfortable.

    c. Not care about it at all.

Fluency Strategy: Predicting the Topic

You can often predict the topic before you read. The topic is the general subject of the text. Look at the title and the pictures in the text. These will give you clues about the topic.

A. Use the strategy to predict the topic. Then skim to check your answer.

    1. Lucky people

    2. Unlucky numbers

    3. Superstitions

B. Read the whole text quickly. Record your reading time in the chart below and on page 169.

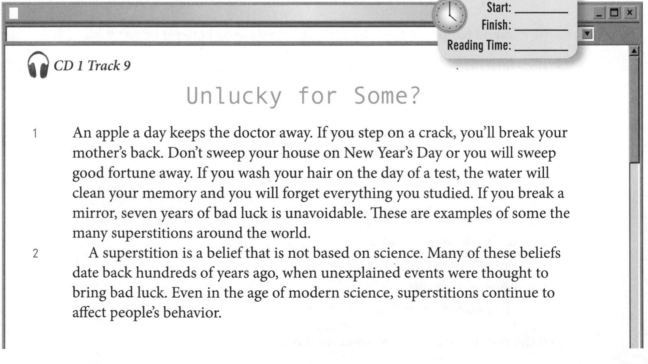

Start: _____
Finish: _____
Reading Time: _____

CD 1 Track 9

Unlucky for Some?

1   An apple a day keeps the doctor away. If you step on a crack, you'll break your mother's back. Don't sweep your house on New Year's Day or you will sweep good fortune away. If you wash your hair on the day of a test, the water will clean your memory and you will forget everything you studied. If you break a mirror, seven years of bad luck is unavoidable. These are examples of some the many superstitions around the world.

2   A superstition is a belief that is not based on science. Many of these beliefs date back hundreds of years ago, when unexplained events were thought to bring bad luck. Even in the age of modern science, superstitions continue to affect people's behavior.

3   Many superstitions are related to numbers. In some Western cultures, the number 13 is thought to be unlucky. Some hotels skip 13 when they number their floors. Friday the thirteenth is seen as an unlucky date in many countries. In China, Japan, and Korea, the word for the number 4 sounds like the word for death, so it is also considered unlucky. In many buildings, the fourth floor is skipped. The floor numbers go from 3 to 5, or the fourth floor is labeled F instead of 4.

4   Superstitions are often linked to everyday objects. In Korea, if a woman holds her chopsticks too close to the tip, she is warned that it will take her a long time to get married. Dropping your chopsticks in China will bring bad luck. If you find an uneven pair of chopsticks at your table, you will miss your next boat, train, or plane.

If you break a mirror, you will have seven years of bad luck.

5   One recent study suggested that people who believe in superstitions actually seem to have more bad luck than other people. For example, people who believe that Friday the thirteenth is unlucky seem to have more accidents on that date. The cause of this bad luck is not the date itself. Instead, say the researchers, people may actually behave differently on that date. People who believe 13 is unlucky may feel more nervous and uncomfortable, which may lead them to drive badly, for example. People who don't believe 13 is unlucky are unaffected.

6   Even people who are not superstitious sometimes stop and think before certain actions. For your next test, do you think washing your hair will make your forget all the answers? Do you want to risk it?

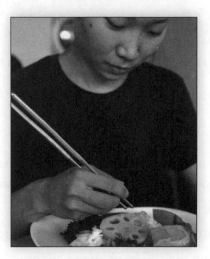

If a woman holds her chopsticks too close to the tip, it will take her a long time to get married.

Checking Fluency and Comprehension

A. Answer the questions. Do not look back at the text.

1. What is the main purpose of the article?
   a. To give examples of study tips.
   b. To describe different superstitions.
   c. To explain why some numbers are unlucky.

2. How do some hotels number their floors?
   a. Eleven, twelve, fourteen, fifteen.
   b. Eleven, twelve, thirteen, fourteen.
   c. Eleven, thirteen, fourteen, fifteen.

3. What do some people believe might happen if you drop your chopsticks?
   a. You might never get married.
   b. You might be late for a flight.
   c. You might have bad luck.

4. Why is the number 4 unlucky in some countries?
   a. Because it is an unlucky date.
   b. Because it is not a floor in many buildings.
   c. Because it sounds like the word for death in some languages.

5. Why do researchers believe people have more accidents on Friday the thirteenth?
   a. Because they are nervous.
   b. Because they have bad luck.
   c. Because they don't believe in good luck.

B. Check your answers with a partner. Record your score on page 169.

Expanding Vocabulary

A. The prefix *un-* gives words the opposite meaning. Scan the text for six words beginning with *un-*. Then use them to complete the definitions.

1. Someone who doesn't feel calm and relaxed is ....

2. If bad things often happen to you, you are ....

3. Something that is not changed by things is ....

4. Something you don't know the reasons for is ....

5. Something you can't stop happening is ....

6. If a set of things are not regular, they are ....

B. **Fill in the blanks. Use the words from A, with or without the prefix *un-*.**

1. I feel so .... on this sofa that I could go to sleep on it.

2. My friend is so .... that she wins things all the time.

3. These pictures look ....—the middle one is higher than the others.

4. Some of the events leading up to the death of Princess Diana are still ....

5. Scott didn't check his essay before he turned it in, so he made some simple and .... mistakes.

6. Many of the houses on our street lost power after the storm but ours was .... so we were fine.

What's Your Opinion?

A. **Do you think these things are lucky or unlucky? Check (✔) your answers.**

	Lucky	Unlucky
1. walking under a ladder	☐	☐
2. finding a cricket in the house	☐	☐
3. sleeping with your head facing north	☐	☐
4. trimming your nails at night	☐	☐
5. knocking on wood	☐	☐

B. **Discuss your answers with a partner.**

Increasing Fluency

Scan the line to find the word on the left. Words may appear more than once. Can you finish in 15 seconds?

	a	b	c	d	e
1. seem	seem	seam	seen	seer	seem
2. close	closer	lose	chose	close	closet
3. floor	flour	floor	four	fool	flood
4. boat	boat	boot	bloat	boat	coat
5. date	bate	late	date	dare	dale
6. sweep	sweet	sleep	swept	sweep	sweep
7. keeps	feeds	keeps	keep	leaps	jeeps
8. break	break	beak	breaks	break	bread

Extensive Reading 3

The Phantom of the Opera

Introduction

This extract from an Oxford *Bookworms* reader gives you the opportunity to read more in English. The more you read, the faster and more fluent you will become. *The Phantom of the Opera* is set in 1880, in the Paris Opera House in France. Everyone is talking about the Phantom of the Opera, the ghost that lives somewhere under the Opera House. Everyone is afraid of the ghost—the singers, the dancers, and the stage workers. But who has actually seen him? The extract you will read begins with one of the dancers telling the others that she has just seen the ghost.

Before Reading

A. What do you think will happen in the extract? Check (✔) your answers.

.... **1.** One of the dancers pretends to be the ghost.

.... **2.** The ghost appears on stage in the middle of a show.

.... **3.** Someone who saw the ghost is found dead.

.... **4.** The opera directors close the Opera House because everyone is afraid of the ghost.

B. Now read the extract to see what happens.

🎧 *CD 1 Track 10*

Words

"Quick! Quick! Close the door! It's him!" Annie Sorelli ran into the dressing room, her face white.

One of the girls ran and closed the door, and then they all turned to Annie Sorelli.

"Who? Where? What's the matter?" they cried.

"It's the ghost!" Annie said. "In the passage. I saw him. He came through the wall in front of me! And…and I saw his face!"   50

Most of the girls were afraid, but one of them, a tall girl with black hair, laughed.

"Pooh!" she said. "Everybody says they see the Opera

ghost, but there isn't really a ghost. You saw a shadow on the wall." But she did not open the door or look into the passage.

"Lots of people see him," a second girl said. "Joseph Buquet saw him two days ago. Don't you remember?"

Then all the girls began to talk at once.

"Joseph says the ghost is tall, and he wears a black evening coat."

"He has the head of a dead man, with a yellow face and no nose…"

"…And no eyes—only black holes!"

Then little Meg Giry spoke for the first time. "Don't talk about him. He doesn't like it. My mother told me."

"Your mother?" the girl with black hair said. "What does your mother know about the ghost?"

"She says that Joseph Buquet is a fool. The ghost doesn't like people talking about him, and one day Joseph Buquet is going to be sorry, very sorry."

"But what does your mother know? Tell us, tell us!" all the girls cried.

"Oh dear!" said Meg. "But please don't say a word to anyone. You know my mother is the doorkeeper for some of the boxes in the Opera House. Well, Box 5 is the ghost's box! He watches the operas from that box, and sometimes he leaves flowers for my mother!"

"The ghost has a box! And leaves flowers in it!"

"Oh, Meg, your mother's telling you stories! How can the ghost have a box?"

"It's true, it's true, I tell you!" Meg said. "Nobody buys tickets for Box 5, but the ghost always comes to it on opera nights."

"So somebody does come there?"

"Why, no!…The ghost comes, but there is nobody there."

The dancers looked at Meg. "But how does your mother know?" one of them asked.

"There's no man in a black evening coat with a yellow face. That's all wrong. My mother never sees the ghost in Box 5, but she hears him! He talks to her, but there is nobody there! And he doesn't like people talking about him!"

But that evening the dancers could not stop talking about the Opera ghost. They talked before the opera, all through

200

250

300

350

400

450

the opera, and after the opera. But they talked very quietly, and they looked behind them before they spoke.

When the opera finished, the girls went back to their dressing room. Suddenly, they heard somebody in the passage, and Madame Giry, Meg's mother, ran into the room. She was a fat, motherly woman, with a red, happy face. But tonight her face was white.

"Oh girls." she cried. "Joseph Buquet is dead! You know he works a long way down, on the fourth floor under the stage. The other stage workers found his dead body there an hour ago—with a rope around his neck!"

"It's the ghost!" cried Meg Giry. "The ghost killed him!"

The Opera House was famous, and the directors of the Opera House were very important men. It was the first week of work for the two new directors, Monsieur Armand Moncharmin and Monsieur Firmin Richard. In the directors' office the next day, the two men talked about Joseph Buquet.

"It was an accident," Monsieur Armand said angrily. "Or Buquet killed himself."

"An accident?...Killed himself?" Monsieur Firmin said. "Which story do you want, my friend? Or do you want the story of the ghost?"

"Don't talk to me about ghosts!" Monsieur Armand said. "We have 1,500 people working for us in this Opera House, and everybody is talking about the ghost. They're all crazy! I don't want to hear about the ghost, OK?"

Extract from *The Phantom of the Opera*, Bookworms Library, Oxford University Press.

500

550

600

650

Total Words: 691

After Reading

Answer the questions.

1. What did Annie see in the passage?

   ....

2. According to Meg's mother, what does the ghost dislike?

   ....

3. What did the ghost leave in the box for Madame Giry?

   ....

4. What did Monsieur Armand Moncharmin think happened to Joseph Buquet?

   ....

Thinking About the Story

Answer the questions.

1. Did you enjoy reading the extract? Do you want to read more about the phantom and the opera house?
2. What do you think happened to Joseph Buquet?
3. What do you think will happen at the opera house?

Timed Repeated Reading

How many words can you read in one minute? Follow the instructions to practice increasing your reading speed.

1. Time yourself. Read the extract for one minute. When you stop, underline the last word you read and write "first" in the margin.
2. Go back to the beginning of the extract. Read again for one minute. Try to read faster this time. When you stop, underline the last word you read and write "second" in the margin.
3. Go back to the beginning of the extract. Read again for one minute. Try to read even faster this time. When you stop, underline the last word you read and write "third" in the margin.
4. Count the number of words you read each time. Record the three numbers on the Timed Repeated Reading Chart on page 169.

Unit 4

Online

Discuss the questions.

1. How much time do you spend each day on a computer?
2. What do you usually use the Internet for?

This unit is about the Internet. In Part 1, you will read about online games. In Part 2, you will read about different ways people use the Internet. The unit is followed by Extensive Reading 4, which is an extract from a book called *The Adventures of Tom Sawyer*. It is about a boy who found ways to have fun before online games were invented.

Part 1   Not All Fun and Games?

Before Reading

Read the statements. Check (✔) any you agree with.

.... **1.** Playing online games is fun.

.... **2.** Playing online games is dangerous.

.... **3.** It is easier to feel successful playing online games than it is in real life.

Comprehension Strategy: Recognizing Points of View

A point of view is an opinion. In some texts, the writer expresses his or her own opinion. In others, the writer summarizes other people's points of view instead. Look for words like *according to, says, believes,* and *thinks.*

A. Read the text. Use the strategy to match the people with the points of view 1–3 above. There is one extra person.

  .... **a.** Jane Abbott   .... **c.** Dr. James Brown

  .... **b.** Jeong-Suk Kim   .... **d.** experts in the gaming industry

B. Read the text again and answer the questions that follow.

🎧 *CD 1 Track 11*

Not All Fun and Games?

1   The number of people playing online games could soon reach 100 million people worldwide, according to a new report by experts in the industry. That is a huge increase from just a few years ago. As the number of people playing online games increases, there are growing concerns about the impact of this trend.

2   Jane Abbott is the mother of two teenage gamers who have skipped school to go to Internet cafes and play online. "I think online games should be banned," she says. "They are dangerous, and are hurting an entire generation of young people." Abbott has told her 17- and 14-year-old sons to stop playing. She tried grounding them. But they still sneak out to an Internet cafe to play the games.

3   According to Jeong-Suk Kim, a skillful gamer, online games are harmless fun. She and her brother often play games online. She says she is able to keep a

balance between gaming and other parts of her life. When she was studying for university entrance examinations, she only played once a week. She has since been accepted by one of the top universities. Now she is back online, playing three or four hours each day.

4   Felipe Gomez found it harder to resist the world of online gaming. "I ended up giving up everything in the real world," he explains. "I spent 20 hours online every day. I entered the unreal world. I didn't want to go out. I stopped eating properly. I just ate junk food in front of the computer. I stopped hanging out with my friends. I played through the night. My girlfriend got tired of it, and we split up. I was so focused on the unreal world that my real life became empty."

5   There may be many reasons why young people become addicted to online games. Dr. James Brown, who studies the issue, believes that the games give people a chance to prove themselves. He says that doing well in these games gives players a real sense of achievement. They can become the center of their virtual universe. This feeling of success may be harder to find in the real world, where many teenagers face exam stress and other problems.

6   Jeong-Suk Kim gives another reason for the attraction of gaming. "Gaming helps me relax at the end of a hard day. In the end it's no different from reading a book or watching TV to relax or hanging out with your friends at the mall."

Checking Comprehension

A. These sentences are false. Complete the new sentences with correct information.

1. More than 100 million people could soon be addicted to online games.
   More than 100 million people ....

2. Jane Abbott's sons don't play online games any more.
   Jane Abbott's sons ....

3. Jeong-Suk Kim failed her university examinations.
   Jeong-Suk Kim ....

4. Some reasons why people are addicted to gaming are given in Paragraph 4.
   Some reasons why people are addicted to gaming are given in ....

5. Felipe Gomez's girlfriend split up with him because he was hanging out with his friends all the time.
   Felipe Gomez's girlfriend split up with him because ....

   ....

6. Dr. James Brown says online games give people a chance to fail.
   Dr. James Brown says online games give people a chance to ....

B. Mark these statements as opinions (O) or facts (F).

...... 1. More than 100 million people could be soon be playing online games.

...... 2. Online games should be banned.

...... 3. Jeong-Suk Kim has been accepted by a top university.

...... 4. Felipe Gomez spent 20 hours online every day.

...... 5. Dr. James Brown studies the issue of online addiction.

...... 6. Gaming is no different from watching TV to relax.

Looking at Vocabulary in Context

A. Find the words in bold in the text. For each line, circle the word that does not belong.

1. **concerns** (par. 1)	hopes	worries	fears
2. **trend** (par. 1)	tendency	development	tradition
3. **banned** (par. 2)	permitted	allowed	let
4. **grounding** (par. 2)	praising	disciplining	punishing
5. **sneak out** (par. 2)	leave secretly	slip away	stay around
6. **addicted** (par. 5)	hooked	bored	obsessed

B. Fill in the blanks with the words in bold from A. Be sure to use the correct forms.

1. South Africa was the first country to .... smoking in all public areas.

2. I think I'm .... to coffee because I drink six cups every day.

3. Valerie tried to .... of her house to see a movie, but her father saw her as she was leaving.

4. The nuclear power station was shut down because of safety ....

5. Amy told her son that he could not go out at night because he was ....

6. Pop stars often start the latest hair and clothing ....

What's Your Opinion?

A. Answer the questions for yourself.

	You	Your Partner
1. Do you like to play online games?	....	....
2. Do you know someone who is addicted to online games?	....	....
3. Do you think online games help people make friends?	....	....
4. Do you like outdoor activities more than using computers?	....	....
5. Do you think there should be a limit to how long teenagers play online games?	....	....

B. Ask a partner the same questions. Discuss your answers. Give reasons for your answers.

Before Reading

Check (✔) the things you do on the Internet.

...... use email   ...... buy things

...... download music   ...... do research for school

Fluency Strategy: Ignoring Unknown Words

To understand what the writer is saying, you don't need to know the meaning of every word. Put your dictionary away. When you come to words you don't know, ignore them. Keep reading. Think about what you *can* understand, not what you can't.

A. **Use the strategy to read the text. Mark these statements true (T), false (F), or don't know (?).**

...... **1.** The article is about the history of the Internet.

...... **2.** Linda Santos doesn't use the Internet to pay bills anymore.

...... **3.** Lee Mun Wu loves the Internet.

...... **4.** Owen O'Neil had a problem buying a camera.

B. **Read the whole text quickly. Record your reading time below and in the chart on page 169.**

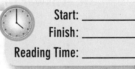

Start: _____
Finish: _____
Reading Time: _____

🎧 *CD 1 Track 12*

The Internet: How Secure Is It?

1   The Internet is used to buy and sell products, pay bills, and communicate with friends and coworkers. But how secure is the information you send over the web? How easy is it for other people to have access to your personal information? *Interactions* Magazine asked four Internet users about their experiences.

2   **Linda Santos, 29, nurse:** I pay all my bills online. One day, I received an email from my bank. It told me that someone was trying to withdraw money from my account, so I should email my password to the "bank official." I felt something was wrong, so I called my bank and asked about the email. The bank said they never sent it. It was an identity thief trying to take money from my account. I'll continue paying my bills this way, but I'll be careful and watch out for scams.

3

Emily Adams, 22, office worker: I was at work, and I sent an email to a friend of mine. I was telling her all about this guy in our office that I secretly liked, Mark. A few minutes later, a friend of Mark's came over to my desk. He said, "So I hear you like Mark?" I was so embarrassed. I couldn't figure out how he knew. It turned out I'd hit the wrong name on my address list, and the email went to someone else instead of my friend. It was my own fault, but I'll look over my emails more carefully before I click "Send" next time.

4   **Lee Mun Wu, 21, university student:** I love the Internet! I look up lots of information online. I also download music. I often buy things through Internet auction websites—furniture, clothes, accessories, CDs, even diet foods. Some things are new but often they are secondhand and very cheap. I have also sold some of my things on Internet auctions. I only use sites I trust and I've never had a problem with security.

5   **Owen O'Neil, 26, artist:** I'm nervous about using the Internet after my experience with one website. The site was for people to buy and sell their things. I saw a digital camera for half price. I paid money into the guy's bank account and waited for the camera to arrive. It never showed up. I called the person and found out the telephone number was not in use. I checked the bank account but it was also not in use. I was cheated! Next time I want a camera I'll go to the store.

Checking Fluency and Comprehension

A. **Complete the sentences. Do not look back at the text.**

1. The article is mainly about ....
   - **a.** how people pay bills online
   - **b.** what people think of Internet security

2. Linda got an email from an .... telling her to email her password.
   - **a.** identity thief
   - **b.** official at her bank

3. Emily was embarrassed because she ....
   - **a.** told a friend she liked someone
   - **b.** sent an email to the wrong person

4. Lee likes to buy things on auction websites, and he has never ....
   - **a.** sold things online
   - **b.** had a security problem

5. Owen bought a camera online, but ....
   - **a.** he never received it
   - **b.** the camera was broken

B. **Check your answers with a partner. Record your score on page 169.**

Expanding Vocabulary

A. **Verbs with two or more parts are called phrasal verbs. Find the phrasal verbs in bold in the text. Then match the halves of the definitions.**

.... 1. If you **watch out for** something (par. 2),   **b.** you examine it carefully.

.... 2. If you **figure** something **out** (par. 3),   **c.** you discovered something.

.... 3. If you **look over** something (par. 3),   **a.** you search for information online or in a book.

.... 4. If you **look** something **up** (par. 4),   **d.** you try to be careful of possible danger.

.... 5. If something **showed up** (par. 5),   **e.** you solve a problem by thinking about it.

.... 6. If you **found out** something (par. 5),   **f.** it appeared or arrived.

B. Fill in the blanks with the words in bold from A. Be sure to use the correct forms.

1. I waited for my friend for half an hour before she finally ....

2. Tom doesn't know where the party is, but he can .... from his sister.

3. We've lost the cab company's phone number, so I'll have to .... it .... in the phone book.

4. In the area by the station you should .... thieves and keep your money hidden.

5. You should always .... your essays before you hand them in to the teacher.

6. I had trouble adding up the bill, but I finally .... it ....

What's Your Opinion?

A. Would you buy these things online? Check (✔) your answers.

	Yes	No	Maybe
1. a camera	☐	☐	☐
2. furniture	☐	☐	☐
3. clothes	☐	☐	☐
4. a car	☐	☐	☐
5. food	☐	☐	☐

B. Discuss your answers with a partner. Give reasons for your answers.

Increasing Fluency

Scan the line to find the word on the left. Words may appear more than once. Can you finish in 15 seconds?

	a	b	c	d	e
1. thing	think	thing	thin	thing	fling
2. mine	mine	mind	mine	miner	nine
3. send	mend	bend	fend	send	send
4. look	lock	hook	look	cook	looks
5. never	never	ever	never	sever	nerve
6. easy	busy	easy	east	easier	easy
7. click	lick	slick	click	click	crick
8. bank	bank	rank	dank	bonk	bank

Extensive Reading 4

The Adventures of Tom Sawyer

Introduction

This extract from an Oxford *Bookworms* reader gives you the opportunity to read more in English. The more you read, the faster and more fluent you will become. *The Adventures of Tom Sawyer* is set in America in the 19th century. The story is about the adventures of a boy, Tom Sawyer, and his friends. The extract you will read starts with Tom's Aunt Polly looking everywhere for Tom. She wants him to paint a fence instead of playing with his friends. But Tom always prefers to play with his friends than to work.

Before Reading

A. **What do you think will happen in the extract? Check (✔) your answers.**

.... **1.** Tom will paint the fence for Aunt Polly.

.... **2.** Tom will play with his friends instead of painting the fence.

.... **3.** Tom's friends will paint most of the fence for him.

.... **4.** Tom will play computer games instead of painting the fence.

B. **Now read the extract to see what happens.**

🎧 *CD 1 Track 13*

Words

> "Tom! *Tom!* Where are you?"
>   No answer.
>   "Where is that boy? When I find him, I'm going to…"
>   Aunt Polly looked under the bed. Then she opened the door and looked out into the garden.
>   *"Tom!"*
>   She heard something behind her. A small boy ran past, but Aunt Polly put out her hand and stopped him.
>   "Ah, there you are! And what's that in your pocket?"
>   "Nothing, Aunt Polly."
>   "Nothing! It's an apple! I can see it. Now listen, Tom. Those apples are not for you, and I—"
>   "Oh, Aunt Polly! Quick—look behind you!"

50

So Aunt Polly looked, and Tom was out of the house in a second. She laughed quietly. "I never learn. I love that Tom, my dead sister's child, but he isn't an easy boy for an old lady. Well, it's Saturday tomorrow. There's no school, but it isn't going to be a holiday for Tom. Oh no! He's going to *work* tomorrow!"

Saturday was a beautiful day. It was summer, the sun was hot, and there were flowers in all the gardens. It was a day for everybody to be happy.

Tom came out of his house with a brush and a big bucket of white paint in his hand. He looked at the fence; it was three meters high and thirty meters long. He put his brush in the paint and painted some of the fence. He did it again. Then he stopped and looked at the fence, put down his brush, and sat down. There were hours of work in front of him, and he was the unhappiest boy in the town.

After ten minutes Tom had an idea, a wonderful idea. He took up the brush again and began work. He saw his friend Joe Harper in the street, but he didn't look at him.

Joe had an apple in his hand. He came up to Tom and looked at the fence.

"I *am* sorry, Tom."

Tom said nothing. The paint brush moved up and down.

"Working for your aunt?" said Joe. "I'm going down to the river. I'm sorry you can't come with me."

Tom put down his brush. "You call this work?" he said.

"Painting a fence?" said Joe. "Of course it's work!"

"Maybe it is and maybe it isn't. But I like it," said Tom. "I can go to the river any day. I can't paint a fence very often."

Joe watched Tom for about five minutes. Tom painted very slowly and carefully. He often stopped, moved back from the fence, and looked at his work with a smile. Joe began to get very interested and said:

"Tom, can I paint a little?"

Tom thought for a second. "I'm sorry, Joe. You see, my aunt wants me to do it because I'm good at painting. My brother Sid wanted to paint, too, but she said no."

"Oh, please, Tom, just a little. I'm good at painting, too. Hey, do you want some of my apple?"

"No, Joe, I can't—"

"OK, you can have *all* my apple!"

Tom gave Joe the brush. He did not smile, but for the first time that day he was a very happy boy. He sat down and ate Joe's apple.

More friends came to laugh at Tom, but soon they all wanted to paint, too. By the afternoon Tom had three balls, an old knife, a cat with one eye, an old blue bottle, and a lot of other exciting things. He was the richest boy in St. Petersburg, and the fence—all thirty meters of it— was a beautiful white. He went back to the house.

"Aunt Polly! Can I go and play now?"

Aunt Polly came out of the house to look. When she saw the beautiful white fence, she was very pleased. She took Tom into the house and gave him an apple.

"Well, you can go and play. But don't come home late."

Tom quickly took a second apple and ran off.

Extract from *The Adventures of Tom Sawyer,* Bookworms Library, Oxford University Press.

450

500

550

600

650

Total Words: 664

After Reading

Answer the questions.

1. Did Tom paint the whole fence by himself?

   ....

2. Did Joe want to paint the fence when he first saw Tom?

   ....

3. Did Tom ask his friends to paint the fence?

   ....

4. Why did Aunt Polly give Tom an apple?

   ....

Thinking About the Story

Answer the questions.

1. Did you enjoy reading the extract? Do you want to read more about Tom's adventures?
2. Do you like Tom? Why or why not?
3. Do you think Tom likes to work?

Timed Repeated Reading

How many words can you read in one minute? Follow the instructions to practice increasing your reading speed.

1. Time yourself. Read the extract for one minute. When you stop, underline the last word you read and write "first" in the margin.
2. Go back to the beginning of the extract. Read again for one minute. Try to read faster this time. When you stop, underline the last word you read and write "second" in the margin.
3. Go back to the beginning of the extract. Read again for one minute. Try to read even faster this time. When you stop, underline the last word you read and write "third" in the margin.
4. Count the number of words you read each time. Record the three numbers on the Timed Repeated Reading Chart on page 169.

Unit 5

Culture

Discuss the questions.

1. If someone from another country came to study in your country, what would you tell them about your culture?

2. Have you ever had a teacher who was from another country? If so, was he or she very different from your other teachers?

This unit is about learning about different cultures. In Part 1, you will read about someone who was a student in a different country. In Part 2, you will read about someone who was a teacher in a different country. The unit is followed by Extensive Reading 5, which is an extract from a book called *Pocahontas*. It is about Englishmen moving to North America in the 1600s and finding a very different culture there.

Learning in America

Before Reading

Discuss the questions.

1. In your school, how are the teachers usually dressed?

2. Do you often ask your teacher questions in class?

Comprehension Strategy: Recognizing Reference Words

We use reference words instead of repeating the names of people, places, ideas, or other things. Look out for common reference words like *it, them, this, that,* etc. Look at sentences nearby to find what they refer to. They can refer to one word or a group of words.

A. **Read the text. Use the strategy to find what these words refer to.**

1. himself (par. 1) ....

2. this (par. 2) ....

3. it (par. 3) ....

4. this (par. 4) ....

5. they (par. 5) ....

6. each other (par. 6) ....

B. **Read the text again and answer the questions that follow.**

🎧 *CD 1 Track 14*

Learning in America

1   I still remember my first class in an American university, *Psychology I*. The professor came into the room very casually dressed, with a cup of coffee in his hand, saying "Hello, everyone". Then he sat on the desk at the front of the room and crossed his legs. He introduced himself and the course.

2   All of this was new to me. In my university in Korea, the professors would be dressed formally, in a suit and tie. They would never bring any drinks into class, and would never sit on a desk!

3   As days went by, I found more differences. For example, I noticed that the students would often interrupt the professor to ask questions. The professor did not seem frustrated by this. Each time a question was asked, he would answer it patiently.

4   One day a student asked the professor exactly the same question another student had asked a few minutes earlier. In my university, if that happened, the professor would say, "I just answered the same question a few minutes ago. Weren't you listening? I hope you'll pay more attention to what is going on in class." However, the professor did not say anything like this. To my surprise, he just answered the question.

5   At first I was confused. I was impressed by the patience of the professors. But at the same time, I was frustrated by all the interruptions. I felt that a lot of time was wasted. The students should listen to the lecture more carefully, I thought. In Korea, students wouldn't interrupt the professor in the middle of a lecture. They would not want to be rude.

6   However, as I spent more time there, I began to learn that in the United States, education is more interactive. There is more room for discussion. Students are encouraged to learn from each other as well as from the teachers. While I missed the respect shown to the teachers in my university in Korea, I enjoyed the freedom and the interactions between professors and students in the American university.

7   All in all, during my stay at an American university, I got more than a degree. I learned about differences in cultures and different ways to look at things, which greatly influenced my life.

An American university class.

Checking Comprehension

Complete the sentences.

1. The author of this article is from ....
   a. the United States.
   b. Canada.
   c. Korea.

2. The author expected the American professor to be .... when students interrupted him.
   a. casual
   b. frustrated
   c. patient

3. The author was surprised that the American professor responded to students' questions by ....
   a. answering them patiently.
   b. answering them after class.
   c. not answering them.

4. The author says students in Korea wouldn't interrupt the professor with questions because they ....
   a. think it is rude.
   b. listen more carefully than American students.
   c. don't want to waste class time.

5. The author feels that in the United States ....
   a. students don't learn as much as they do in Korea.
   b. students show more respect to their teachers than in Korea.
   c. there is more discussion in class.

6. The author now feels ....
   a. the classes in the Korean university were better than in the United States.
   b. the classes in the American university were better than in Korea.
   c. there were good things about the classes in both universities.

Looking at Vocabulary in Context

A. Find the words in bold in the text. Mark the statements true (T) or false (F).

...... 1. If someone is **casually** (par. 1) dressed, they are probably wearing a suit and tie.

...... 2. If you **interrupt** (par. 3) someone, you stop them from what they are doing.

...... 3. A **frustrated** (par. 3) person is usually calm and patient.

...... 4. If someone admires and respects you, they are probably **impressed** (par. 5) with you.

...... 5. **Interactive** (par. 6) activities involve two-way communication.

...... 6. If something **influenced** (par. 7) you, it had no effect on you.

B. Fill in the blanks with the words from A. Be sure to use the correct forms.

1. I was really .... with your performance. I didn't realize you were so talented.

2. You can dress .... here. It is fine to wear jeans and T-shirts.

3. Picasso has really .... my style of painting.

4. I could not finish watching the movie because my little brother .... me.

5. I feel .... when I have to wait in long lines at stores.

6. The children enjoyed participating in the .... games at the science museum.

What's Your Opinion?

A. Answer the questions for yourself.

	You	Your Partner
1. Do you think professors should dress formally?	....	....
2. Do you learn better in a quiet class?	....	....
3. Do you think your culture is more polite than others?	....	....
4. Do you think it's OK to interrupt your teacher?	....	....
5. Do you learn from your classmates and your teachers?	....	....

B. Ask a partner the same questions. Discuss your answers. Give reasons for your answers.

Part 2 A Team Player

Before Reading

Discuss the questions.

1. Do you prefer to make decisions on your own or as part of a team?
2. Do you think your classes are the same as classes in other countries?

Fluency Strategy: Skimming for the Main Ideas

Skimming is reading fast to understand the writer's main idea, or message. Read the title, the first paragraph, and the first sentences in the other paragraphs. Then read the last paragraph. Read quickly; details are not important.

A. Use the strategy to skim the text. Circle the main idea.

1. I taught English for a year in Japan.
2. Being a team player is very important in Japanese culture.
3. There are lots of differences between Australia and Japan.

B. Read the whole text quickly. Record your reading time in the chart below and on page 169.

Start: _____
Finish: _____
Reading Time: _____

CD 1 Track 15

A Team Player

1   I am an Australian teacher at a high school in Sydney. I teach English as a second language. A couple of years ago, I went to Japan to teach English at a high school for one year. I quickly realized that schools in the two countries are very different.

2   In my first class, I put the students in groups, and asked them to discuss the question on the blackboard, "Who has more advantages in society: men or women?" In my class in Australia, this topic would get everyone talking. Even though the students would make lots of mistakes with English, each one wanted to say what they thought. For me, this meant a successful lesson— everyone was speaking in English. So, when I tried the same lesson with my Japanese students, I was confident that the same thing would happen.

3   I was wrong. Instead of a noisy debate with different viewpoints, there was almost silence. The students whispered briefly and quietly within their groups. Then a spokesperson gave one answer for the group. Instead of each student expressing his or her individual opinion, they had reached agreement as a group.

4   I was surprised at the time, but I now realize that the students were acting as a team. In my year in Japan, I came to understand what being a team player means. A team player thinks of others before she thinks of herself. A good team player puts herself last, and puts her teammates first. It is the group–the family, classmates, colleagues–before the individual. Decisions are best made by the group, not the individual.

5   Learning how to be a good team player in Japan begins at an early age. In a class, children are often organized into groups and taught how to study or play together. This emphasis on being a good team player continues in the work place and in all aspects of society.

6   This team playing idea is very different from Australian culture. In Australia, it is the individual who is important, not the group. I was taught from a very early age to make my own decisions, to become my own person. At first, I did not really understand the Japanese way of thinking about team playing. I felt that Australian culture was better. But, after a year in Japan, I learned that cultures are different, and that it is not a question of which one is better.

Checking Fluency and Comprehension

A. **Answer the questions. Do not look back at the text.**

1. The author teaches English in ....
   a. Japan.   **b.** America.   **c.**   Australia.

2. A good team player thinks of the .... first.
   a. individual   **b.** group   **c.** teacher

3. Japanese people start learning to be a team player ....
   a. in college   **b.** when they are very young   **c.** when they get a job

4. In the author's classes in Australia, students usually offer many different
   ....
   a. advantages.   **b.** topics.   **c.** opinions.

5. The author's lesson in team playing taught her about ....
   a. cultural differences.   **b.** why Australia is better.   **c.** why Japan is better.

B. **Check your answers with a partner. Record your score on page 169.**

Expanding Vocabulary

A. **Compound nouns are words made from two words. The words in bold are each part of a compound noun. Find the complete compound nouns in the text and fill in the blanks. Then match them with the definitions.**

.... **1.** .... **school** (par. 1)	**a.** something a teacher writes on
.... **2.** .... **board** (par. 2)	**b.** the school you go to before college
.... **3. view** .... (par. 3)	**c.** people in the same class as you
.... **4.** .... **player** (par. 4)	**d.** someone who works well in a team
.... **5.** .... **mates** (par. 4)	**e.** opinions
.... **6. class** .... (par. 4)	**f.** people on the same team as you

B. Fill in the blanks with the words from A.

1. When David Beckham scored the winning goal, all his .... ran over to congratulate him.

2. I know I need glasses because I can't read the ....

3. Students need to pass a test before they can graduate from ....

4. At work, I prefer to do things on my own, so I'm not really a good ....

5. All of my .... are 16 or 17, so I am the youngest in the class.

6. I've told you all what I think, but I'm happy to hear some different ....

What's Your Opinion?

A. Do you agree or disagree with these statements? Check (✔) your answers.

	Agree	Disagree
1. I think I can learn a lot from other cultures.	☐	☐
2. I think the individual is more important than the group.	☐	☐
3. I think my culture is better than other cultures.	☐	☐
4. I am a team player.	☐	☐
5. I am sometimes surprised by the way people from other cultures act.	☐	☐

B. Discuss your answers with a partner. Give reasons for your answers.

Increasing Fluency

Scan the line to find the word on the left. Words may appear more than once. Can you finish in 15 seconds?

	a	b	c	d	e
1. team	tea	team	beam	seem	teams
2. player	player	players	player	play	prayer
3. high	high	sigh	right	thigh	high
4. better	setter	letter	better	netter	better
5. same	sane	fame	name	same	came
6. early	yearly	easy	really	early	nearly
7. meant	meant	neat	meat	mean	meant
8. begins	benign	begin	begins	design	begun

Extensive Reading 5

Pocahontas

Introduction

This extract from an Oxford *Bookworms* reader gives you the opportunity to read more in English. The more you read, the faster and more fluent you will become. *Pocahontas* is set in North America in 1607. The story is about Englishmen coming to Virginia, America, to start a new life. The native Americans, the Algonquin Indians, are not happy about the Englishmen coming to their country. The extract you will read starts with the Englishmen settling in their new home.

Before Reading

A. What do you think will happen in the extract? Check (✔) your answers.

...... **1.** The Indians try to make friends with the Englishmen.

...... **2.** Many of the Englishmen die.

...... **3.** All of the Englishmen return to England.

...... **4.** The Englishmen build houses with the Indians.

B. Now read the extract to see what happens.

🎧 *CD 1 Track 16*

Words

The Englishmen began to build a little town. They called it Jamestown because the King of England was called James. They called the river James River, too.

The leaders of the Englishmen were Christopher Newport, Edward Wingfield, and John Smith. They wanted to learn more about Virginia, so Smith and Newport took twenty men and went up the river in a small boat.   50

The other men stayed in Jamestown with Wingfield. They began to build houses, and to make gardens and fields outside the town.

"The fields are more important than the houses," said Wingfield. "And we must work quickly because it's nearly   100 summer now. We must have corn and vegetables for the winter."

But it was not easy. The weather was hot, and the men were tired after four months at sea. Some men worked hard, but many sat in the sun, and did nothing. The Indians watched and waited.

Smith and Newport went a hundred kilometers up the river. They visited Indian villages and talked to a lot of Indians. Some of the Indians were friendly, and some were not. When Smith and Newport came back to Jamestown, Wingfield was very pleased to see them.

"I was afraid for you," he said. "But you're not dead!"

"No, of course not," said Smith. "What's the matter?"

"It's the Indians," Wingfield said. "They're trying to kill us. Yesterday, they nearly killed *me*!"

"Well, what did you do?" Smith asked. "Our men have guns, and the Indians are very afraid of guns."

"But there were hundreds of Indians," said Wingfield, "and…we weren't ready. Our guns were on the ships."

"Why?" asked Smith angrily. "The men must always be ready; they must carry their guns with them. The Indians tried to kill you because they weren't afraid of you."

"Yes, but—we must be nice to them," said Wingfield. 300

"We can be friendly, but we must be careful first," said Smith. "We must build good walls around the town, and put the big guns from the ships on them. Then the Indians can't kill us."

For a month everyone worked hard. They built walls 350 around the town and moved the big guns from the ships. But the men were afraid to work in the fields because of the Indians. And the sun got hotter and hotter.

In June Newport went back to England with two of the ships. A hundred and five men stayed in Jamestown. They 400 had very little food. The corn from England was now bad, and the new corn in the fields was not ready. The river water was bad too, and soon many of the men were sick with a fever. Forty-six men died that summer.

Some of the men tried to leave Jamestown and go home 450 in the ship, but Smith stopped them. "We're here to work and to build a new town," he said. "But first, we must find food. There are birds in the sky, fish in the river, animals in the forest—we must kill them and eat them. And we must 500 get corn from the Indians, too. I can do that."

Smith wasn't afraid of the Indians, but he was always very careful. He carried his gun all the time. Most of the Indians were afraid of Smith, but they liked him too. He 550 was friendly, and he loved their beautiful country. And he learned their language because he wanted to talk to them and understand them. Often, he gave the Indians little things from England, and they gave him food.

But when winter came, there were only fifty men alive in Jamestown. They had some food, but they needed more. 600

The Virginian winter is long and cold, and fifty men need a lot of food.

In December Smith went up the river in a boat with nine men. Two of the friendly Indians went with them. It was very cold, and the Englishmen were hungry. But Smith was happy and excited.

"I'm going to find food for Christmas," he said to the men in Jamestown. "Wait for me here, and work hard! This is a beautiful country, and we're going to stay here!"

Extract from *Pocahontas,* Bookworms Library, Oxford University Press.

650

Total Words: 691

After Reading

Answer the questions.

1. Why did the Englishmen call their town Jamestown?

....

2. What did Smith say the men must always carry with them?

....

3. Why did the Indians like Smith?

....

4. What did the Englishmen need in the winter?

....

Thinking About the Story

Answer the questions.

1. Did you enjoy reading the extract? Do you want to read more about John Smith and the Indians in North America?
2. Do you think Smith and his men will stay in Jamestown?
3. Do you think the Englishmen and the Indians will live peacefully together?

Timed Repeated Reading

How many words can you read in one minute? Follow the instructions to practice increasing your reading speed.

1. Time yourself. Read the extract for one minute. When you stop, underline the last word you read and write "first" in the margin.
2. Go back to the beginning of the extract. Read again for one minute. Try to read faster this time. When you stop, underline the last word you read and write "second" in the margin.
3. Go back to the beginning of the extract. Read again for one minute. Try to read even faster this time. When you stop, underline the last word you read and write "third" in the margin.
4. Count the number of words you read each time. Record the three numbers on the Timed Repeated Reading Chart on page 169.

Unit 6

Age

Discuss the questions.

1. Who is the oldest person you know?
2. Why do some people live longer than other people?

This unit is about how long people live. In Part 1, you will read about someone who lived a long life. In Part 2, you will read about a scientist who studies aging. The unit is followed by Extensive Reading 6, which is an extract from a book called *Christmas in Prague*. It is about an old man who has a secret from his past.

Part 1   The Secret to a Long Life

Before Reading

Look at the photo on page 73. Do you think the statements are true (T) or false (F)?

...... **1.** The woman in the photo lived to be 150 years old.

...... **2.** She smoked for over 100 years.

...... **3.** She learned the sport of fencing when she was 85.

Comprehension Strategy: Identifying Meaning From Context

You can often work out the meaning of words you don't know from the words and phrases nearby. Try to work out the part of speech (noun, verb, adjective, adverb) of the new word. Look at the sentences before and after the word. They may use words with the same meaning or with the opposite meaning.

A. **Find the words in bold in the text. Use the strategy to work out the meanings, then circle the answers.**

1. **Life expectancy** (par. 2) means something about *age / birthday parties.*

2. **Gender** (par. 4) means something about *men and women / countries.*

3. **Marital status** (par. 5) means something about *health / marriage.*

B. **Read the text again and answer the questions that follow.**

🎧 *CD 1 Track 17*

The Secret to a Long Life

1   What is the secret to a long life? The oldest known person on record is a French woman, Jeanne Calment. She seemed to disprove the idea that healthy living was the answer. Despite smoking for 100 years, she lived to the age of 122. She believed her long life was thanks to her diet.

2   The average life expectancy for all people in the world today is 63 years. This figure varies widely from country to country. Japan has the world's highest life expectancy; 85 for women and 78 for men. More than 20,000 of its population have celebrated their 100th birthday. Researchers believe part of the reason for this lies in the healthy Japanese diet and their good health care system.

3   People who live in developed countries generally live longer than those who

live in poorer parts of the world. Factors like war, disease, quality of diet, and access to health care all affect life expectancy. When a country's health care and education improve, life expectancy goes up.

4   Another important factor is gender. Women, on average, live longer than men. Over 80 percent of people who live beyond the age of 100 are women. The reasons for this are not fully understood. Some scientists believe that women are born with genes that help them live longer than men. Others argue that men often lead more risky lifestyles that put them at greater chance of dying than women. They have more dangerous jobs. Also, men generally drive more, and also smoke more than women. Men are even killed more often than women.

5   Another area that researchers have looked at is marital status. They have not found a clear difference in life expectancy between married women and single women. However, one British study found that married men appeared to live longer, on average, than single men. This may be because married men tend to have a healthier lifestyle than single men. They eat more healthily, and, on average, take fewer risks.

Jeanne Calment

6   Jeanne Calment did not seem to worry about taking risks. At the age of 85, she learned fencing. At the age of 100, she was still riding a bicycle. She gave up smoking when she was 121, but not for health reasons. She couldn't see clearly enough to light the cigarettes herself, and she was too proud to ask other people to do it for her. Perhaps the secret to her age was that she never got bored with life.

Checking Comprehension

A. Mark the statements true (T) or false (F). Correct the ones which are false.

...... **1.** This article is about what causes people to live a long life.

....

...... **2.** Life expectancy is similar for all people around the world.

....

...... **3.** The food people eat does not affect how long they live.

....

...... **4.** Activities such as driving can affect life expectancy.

....

...... **5.** We don't know for certain why women live longer than men.

....

...... **6.** Jeanne Calment proves the theory that a risky lifestyle lowers life expectancy.

....

B. Fill in the blanks in the chart to show what Jeanne Calment was doing at each age. Write *yes* or *no*.

	Smoking	Fencing	Riding a bicycle
1. 25	....	....	
2. 85	....	....	
3. 100	....		....
4. 121	....		

Looking at Vocabulary in Context

A. Find the words in bold in the text. Circle the correct definitions.

1. If you **disprove** (par. 1) an idea, you show it is *true / false*.

2. **Population** (par. 2) means the *number of people in a particular area / things that people enjoy*.

3. **Developed countries** (par. 3) are countries with *an advanced level of technology / not much technology*.

4. **Genes** (par. 4) are *parts of a cell in humans, animals, and plants / parts of a computer*.

5. A **risky** (par. 4) activity is *safe / unsafe*.

6. Your **lifestyle** (par. 4) is *the clothes you wear / the way you live*.

B. Fill in the blanks with the correct form of the words in A. Be sure to use the correct forms.

1. Good health care and education is available for many people in ....

2. Scientists .... the old belief that the world is flat.

3. Our parents give us .... that determine the color of our hair and eyes.

4. Emma wanted to change her ...., so she quit smoking and joined a gym.

5. The world's .... is expected to reach over eight billion people by 2025.

6. It can be extremely .... to drive during a snowstorm.

What's Your Opinion?

A. How important are these things in determining life expectancy? Number them from 1 (most important) to 5 (least important).

.... education

.... health of parents

.... job

.... diet

.... hobbies

B. Discuss your answers with a partner. Give reasons for your answers.

Before Reading

Discuss the questions.

1. Do you know anyone who is over 100 years old?
2. Would you like to live for 1,000 years? Why or why not?

Fluency Strategy: Recognizing Signal Words

Signal words show how the text is organized. Words like *main*, *key*, or *major* often introduce the most important point. *In addition* and *also* give more information. *However* gives contrasting information.

A. **Scan the text for the signal words. Match them with the information they introduce.**

...... **1.** in addition   **a.** Dr. de Grey's most important argument

...... **2.** however   **b.** Dr. de Grey's second point

...... **3.** main point   **c.** Dr. de Grey's third point

...... **4.** also   **d.** arguments against de Grey

B. **Read the whole text quickly. Record your reading time below and in the chart on page 169.**

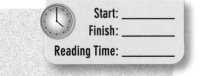

🎧 *CD 1 Track 18*

Start: _____
Finish: _____
Reading Time: _____

A Cure for Aging?

1   (Cambridge, England) Dr. Aubrey de Grey believes that one day it will be possible for humans to live for 1,000 years. Dr. de Grey is a scientist at Cambridge University, England. Many other scientists reject his theory, but he stands by it.

2   Dr. de Grey's main point is that we can control aging. He says aging is caused by damage to the cells of the human body. He believes that if we fix the damaged cells, then we will cure aging. This means that humans will be able to live for 1,000 years, and maybe even longer.

3   In addition, Dr. de Grey believes that people who are 1,000 years old will not be weak. Instead, he says they will be strong and healthy, full of physical and mental energy. Dr. de Grey thinks this is a wonderful possibility. For

Dr. Aubrey de Grey

example, people often have many new ideas and things they want to do, but they die before they can finish them. If they can live for 1,000 years, they will have more time to complete their goals.

Dr. de Grey also believes that it is natural for humans to want to fix things and to change the world. It is unnatural, he says, for humans to accept the world as it is now. He thinks if people live that long, they will work hard to make the world better than it is today.

However, many people disagree with de Grey's ideas. They say that even if we could increase the natural human lifespan, it would not be a good thing. They argue that aging is a natural part of the human experience. If people started to live much longer, the world would have too many people in it. How would we feed everyone when there are so many poor and starving people in the world today? Even if there was an aging cure, they say, it would be so expensive that only rich people could afford it. Finally, they argue that most people would not want to live for that long.

Dr. de Grey is not worried about these arguments. As we live longer, he says, we will have a greater chance of solving the world's problems. We are losing 100,000 people to old age every day. If we can cure aging, he says, we are gaining the chance to save lives. According to Dr. de Grey, that is the most important thing a person can spend their time doing.

Checking Fluency and Comprehension

A. Complete the sentences. Do not look back at the text.

1. The article is mainly about ....

   a. how to live forever.

   b. a scientist and his ideas about aging.

2. Dr. de Grey believes we can live longer if ....

   a. we fix damaged cells.

   b. we solve the world's problems.

3. Most scientists ....

   a. believe in Dr. de Grey's ideas.

   b. don't believe in Dr. de Grey's ideas.

4. Dr. de Grey believes that aging is ....

   a. natural and shouldn't change.

   b. something that can be cured.

5. Dr. de Grey thinks the most important thing to do is to ....

   a. save lives.

   b. help poor people.

B. Check your answers with a partner. Record your score on page 169.

Expanding Vocabulary

A. Find the words in bold in the text. Match them with the definitions. Then find the antonyms of the words in the text.

Word (in text)	Definition	Antonym (in text)
...... 1. **stands by** (par. 1)	a. mend	.... (par. 1)
...... 2. **fix** (par. 2)	b. strange, odd	.... (par. 2)
...... 3. **strong** (par. 3)	c. defends	.... (par. 3)
...... 4. **unnatural** (par. 4)	d. powerful	.... (par. 4)
...... 5. **rich** (par. 5)	e. increasing	.... (par. 5)
...... 6. **gaining** (par. 6)	f. wealthy	.... (par. 6)

B. Fill in the blanks with the words in bold from A or their antonyms. Be sure to use the correct forms.

1. You need to be .... to move that heavy box.

2. Please be careful not to .... that new TV.

3. People who don't exercise often .... weight as they get older.

4. We're too .... to afford eating at expensive restaurants.

5. Even if the voters don't like the president, his supporters will .... him.

6. Most people prefer .... sunlight to electric light.

What's Your Opinion?

A. Do you agree or disagree with the statements? Check (✔) your answers.

	Agree	Disagree
1. It is possible for humans to live much longer than they do now.	☐	☐
2. The world will be better if humans live for 1,000 years.	☐	☐
3. People don't have enough time to complete their goals.	☐	☐
4. There will not be enough food if we live for 1,000 years.	☐	☐
5. It is natural for humans to live about 100 years.	☐	☐

B. Discuss your answers with a partner.

Increasing Fluency

Scan the line to find the word on the left. Words may appear more than once. Can you finish in 15 seconds?

	a	b	c	d	e
1. poor	pool	pour	poor	boor	poor
2. live	life	live	liver	lives	line
3. goals	goals	poles	gores	goals	foals
4. long	song	long	long	loon	lone
5. losing	losing	nosing	rousing	doing	suing
6. die	die	diet	dies	died	lie
7. could	should	could	cold	could	scold
8. cells	cells	cell	sells	spell	sills

Extensive Reading 6

Christmas in Prague

Introduction

This extract from an Oxford *Bookworms* reader gives you the opportunity to read more in English. The more you read, the faster and more fluent you will become. *Christmas in Prague* is set in England and in Prague, in the Czech Republic. The story is about an old man's family secret from the past. The old man is Josef. Josef was born in Prague. He now lives in England with his son, Jan, and his son's wife, Carol. The extract you will read begins with Carol getting an invitation to Prague to play the harp at a concert for Christmas. Will Josef join her in Prague?

Before Reading

A. **What do you think will happen in the extract? Check (✔) your answers.**

.... **1.** Josef wants to go to Prague because he has lots of good memories of it.

.... **2.** Josef doesn't want to go to Prague.

.... **3.** Josef decides to go to Prague one last time.

.... **4.** Josef tells Carol and Jan his secret from the past.

B. **Now read the extract to see what happens.**

🎧 *CD 1 Track 19*

Words

"Hey, Jan, look at this!" Carol said. She had a letter in her hand and took it across to her husband at the breakfast table. "It's from the Oxford Orchestra," she said. "They're giving concerts in the Czech Republic this Christmas. They're doing three concerts in Prague and they're asking me to go because they need a harpist. Shall we go to Prague for Christmas? I can play with the orchestra, and you can come with us."

50

"When are the concerts?" asked Jan. "I always have a lot of work in the weeks before Christmas. I must finish writing my new book then."

100

Jan taught Czech at Oxford University and wrote

books about languages. He was born in Czechoslovakia, but came to England with his father when he was very young. He met Carol when she was one of his students at the university.

"The first concert is on December 20th," Carol answered. "Are you free then?"

"No, I'm sorry, Carol," Jan said, "but I can't come before December 24th."

"Well, it doesn't matter. You can come for the second concert. It's on December 25th."

"But what about my father?" said Jan. "We can't go away and leave him at Christmas time. He loves a family Christmas with us—you know that."

Josef Vlach was sixty-eight years old, and his eyes were bad. He couldn't see very well, so he lived with Carol and Jan.

"Josef can come with us," Carol said. "He often talks about Prague at Christmas. He says it's the most beautiful time of the year there because of all the snow on the old buildings."

"I know," said Jan. "But he only talks about Prague. He never wants to go there. Every time we ask him to come with us, he says no. I don't know why, but I think it's because of my mother. When he thinks about Prague, he remembers her. You know, sometimes he cries when he looks at his photo of her—after all these years!"

Just then the door opened and Jan's father came slowly into the room.

"Good morning," he said, and sat down at the table. "Is there any coffee?"

"It's cold now," said Carol. "Shall I make you some more?"

"Thank you, my dear," he answered. "You're very good to me."

Carol went out for some coffee. Jan looked at his father carefully. "I must ask him now," he thought, "while Carol is out of the room."

400

"You're very quiet, Jan," said the old man. "Is something wrong?"

"No, no," said Jan quickly. "Nothing's wrong. It's just...I want to ask you a question, but I...I...it's difficult."

Jan stopped. His father smiled.

"Difficult? Why is it difficult? Are you afraid of an old man?"

"Of course not," said Jan. "But I *am* afraid of your answer. You see, Carol wants to go very much. She loves playing her harp, but it's Christmas time and—"

"Stop!" said Josef. "What are you talking about? Where does Carol want to go at Christmas?"

"To Prague," said Jan. "And I would like to go with her. We want you to come too."

"Ah!" said the old man. "To Prague. I understand now."

The room was suddenly very quiet. Jan drank his cold coffee and waited.

The old man took something out of his pocket. It was a photograph of his dead wife, Jan's mother. He spoke very quietly—not to Jan, but to the photograph in his hand.

"Perhaps now...before I die...just once I can go back again..."

Carol came back with some hot coffee. She looked at Josef, then at Jan.

"Shhh...He's thinking about Prague," Jan said quietly.

Carol put the coffee on the table and sat down. The hands on the clock slowly moved through two long minutes. Then the old man put the photograph back in his pocket.

"All right," he said. "Let's all go to Prague for Christmas. It's beautiful there when it snows. I remember it so well... so very well."

Extract from *Christmas in Prague,* **Bookworms Library, Oxford University Press.**

After Reading

Answer the questions.

1. What is Carol's job?

   ....

2. Why does Josef live with Jan and Carol?

   ....

3. Why did Jan think Josef might not want to go to Prague?

   ....

4. What does Josef take out of his pocket?

   ....

Thinking About the Story

Answer the questions.

1. Did you enjoy reading the extract? Do you want to read more about Carol, Jan, and Josef?
2. What do you think happened to Josef's wife?
3. Do you think they will all have a happy Christmas in Prague?

Timed Repeated Reading

How many words can you read in one minute? Follow the instructions to practice increasing your reading speed.

1. Time yourself. Read the extract for one minute. When you stop, underline the last word you read and write "first" in the margin.
2. Go back to the beginning of the extract. Read again for one minute. Try to read faster this time. When you stop, underline the last word you read and write "second" in the margin.
3. Go back to the beginning of the extract. Read again for one minute. Try to read even faster this time. When you stop, underline the last word you read and write "third" in the margin.
4. Count the number of words you read each time. Record the three numbers on the Timed Repeated Reading Chart on page 169.

Survivors

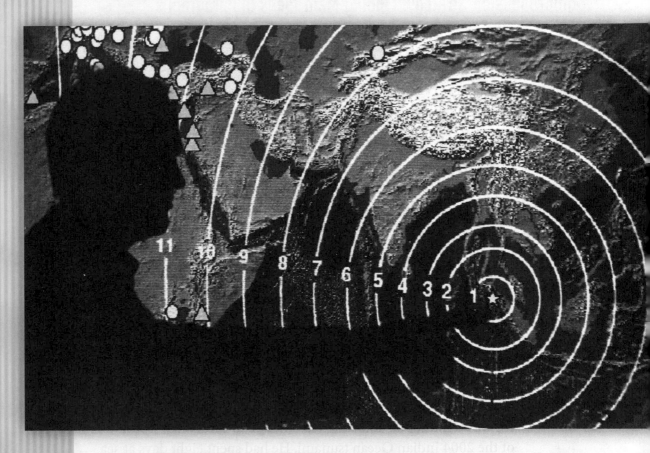

Discuss the questions.

1. Which countries did the 2004 tsunami hit?
2. Do you know any stories of people who survived a natural disaster?

This unit is about survivors of the 2004 tsunami. In Part 1, you will read about a man who survived for eight days at sea. In Part 2, you will read about a friendship that started between two survivors. The unit is followed by Extensive Reading 7, which is an extract from a book called *The Wizard of Oz*. It is about a little girl who survives a big storm that takes her to a strange place.

Before Reading

Discuss the questions.

1. How long do you think someone could survive in the ocean without a boat?
2. How would someone find water to drink in the middle of the ocean?

Comprehension Strategy: Finding Main Ideas in Paragraphs

Every paragraph has a main idea. This is the most important thing the writer wants to say. The main idea is often near the beginning of the paragraph.

A. Read the text. Write the paragraph number with its main idea.

4. **a.** The tsunami was caused by an earthquake under the ocean.
...... **b.** The tsunami had a terrible impact on many countries.
...... **c.** A man survived the tsunami after eight days at sea.
...... **d.** Rizal is making a new life for himself.
...... **e.** Rizal survived by holding onto a tree, drinking rainwater, and eating coconuts.
...... **f.** Aceh was one of the areas hit very badly by the tsunami.

B. Read the text again and answer the questions that follow.

🎧 *CD 2 Track 2*

Survival After Eight Days at Sea

1   In January 2005, an amazing picture appeared on newspaper front pages around the world. It was a photo of a man drifting in the middle of the ocean. He was standing on a floating tree. The man, Rizal Shah Putra, was a survivor of the 2004 Indian Ocean tsunami. He had spent eight days at sea.

2   Rizal was cleaning a mosque in Aceh, Indonesia, when the tsunami struck on December 26, 2004. Just before the tsunami destroyed his village, he says, he heard warning calls. But it was too late for him to run to higher ground. The huge waves swept him out to sea. He spent hours fighting the raging water. Just as he was about to give up, he saw a tree floating near him. He managed to reach it and hold on. He held onto the tree for eight days. He said he thought each day would be his last. He survived by drinking rainwater and eating coconuts he found floating in the water. He cracked them open with a

Rizal Shah Putra

doorknob. On the eighth day, sailors on a passing ship saw him and rescued him. The strong currents from the tsunami had carried him almost 160 kilometers from shore.

3   The tsunami was one of the worst natural disasters in history. It affected many countries, including Indonesia, Thailand, Sri Lanka, India, and Tanzania. Over 250,000 people were killed. Coastal areas were devastated. Thousands drowned in their homes or on beaches. Houses and land were destroyed. Over three million people lost their jobs. Millions more became homeless.

4   The tsunami was caused by a huge earthquake under the Indian Ocean. The earthquake caused a huge wave, which moved across the ocean at the speed of a jet plane. When the tsunami struck land, the waves were up to 15 meters high.

5   Rizal came from one of the areas worst hit by the tsunami. He and his family lived in the Indonesian province of Aceh, at the tip of Sumatra. Rizal's parents, brother, and sister were all lost in the disaster. Whole towns and villages in the area were destroyed. In some villages more than 70 percent of the people died. The Asian Development Bank says that about 44 percent of people in Aceh lost their jobs.

6   Rizal is rebuilding his life. In 2005, he decided to continue his studies at a university in Malaysia. He says he is now living his second life.

Checking Comprehension

A. Number the events in the order they happened to Rizal from 1 to 8.

...... **a.** He started studying at a university in Malaysia.

...... **b.** He was cleaning a mosque.

...... **c.** He was seen by sailors on a ship.

...... **d.** He caught hold of a tree.

...... **e.** He ate coconuts and drank rainwater.

...... **f.** He was washed out to sea.

...... **g.** He heard villagers calling warnings.

...... **h.** He was rescued.

B. Answer the questions.

1. How far was Rizal from land when he was rescued?

   ....

2. Did Rizal think he would survive when he was on the tree?

   ....

3. Which countries were affected by the tsunami?

   ....

4. How many people in these countries became unemployed as a result of the tsunami?

   ....

5. What caused the tsunami?

   ....

6. What happened in the province of Aceh?

   ....

Looking at Vocabulary in Context

A. **Find the words in bold in the text. Circle the correct definitions.**

1. If something is **drifting** (par. 1), it is *moving with no control or direction / moving quickly to its destination.*

2. A **mosque** (par. 2) is a *mountain / place of religious worship.*

3. If something **struck** (par. 2) you, it *crashed into / went away from* you.

4. If a place is **devastated** (par. 3), it is *damaged a little bit / damaged very badly.*

5. If someone **drowned** (par. 3), they *died in water / died from hunger.*

6. If something is **destroyed** (par. 3), it is *newly made / broken so it can't be used.*

B. **Fill in the blanks with the words from A. Be sure to use the correct forms.**

1. The car went off the road and .... a tree but no one was hurt.

2. My sister nearly .... after she fell off her surfboard, but someone rescued her.

3. Most of my CDs were .... by the fire.

4. My hat fell into the water and .... slowly down the river.

5. Many African countries have been .... by war and disease.

6. People must take off their shoes before they pray in the ....

What's Your Opinion?

A. **Do you agree or disagree with the statements? Check (✔) your answers.**

	Agree	Disagree	Not Sure
1. I would know what to do if a tsunami hit.	☐	☐	☐
2. I think bad experiences can make people stronger.	☐	☐	☐
3. I think bad experiences damage people for the rest of their lives.	☐	☐	☐
4. I would be so frightened in an emergency, I wouldn't know what to do.	☐	☐	☐
5. I would be able to control my feelings in an emergency and deal with it calmly.	☐	☐	☐

B. **Discuss your answers with a partner. Give reasons for your answers.**

Before Reading

Discuss the questions.

1. How did you meet your best friend?
2. Are you and your best friend similar or very different?

Fluency Strategy: Predicting the Topic

You can often predict the topic before you read. The topic is the general subject of the text. Look at the title and the pictures in the text. These will give you clues about the topic.

A. **Use the strategy to predict the topic. Then skim to check your answer.**

1. Protecting animals in Africa.
2. Friendship between a pair of animals.
3. Friendship between an animal and a person.

B. **Read the whole text quickly. Record your reading time below and in the chart on page 169.**

🎧 *CD 2 Track 3*

Start: _____
Finish: _____
Reading Time: _____

An Unlikely Friendship

1   Owen and Mzee are friends. At first sight, they seem like an unlikely pair. For a start, there is the age difference. Mzee is over 130 years old. Owen is just two. There is also the fact that Mzee is a tortoise and Owen is a hippo.

2   The story of their friendship began in the East African country of Kenya. In December 2004, on the day before the tsunami, heavy rains suddenly washed a group of hippos down a river and out to sea. The next day the tsunami washed the hippos back up the river—all except one. The hippo that was left behind was a baby. He had somehow become separated from his family.

3   People on the beach saw the baby hippo in the ocean, not far from shore. He was trying to get to the beach, but the waves were too high. They decided to rescue the hippo. Using boats, nets, and cars, they managed to drag the tired animal out of the ocean. They named him Owen after one of the people who saved him.

4   Owen was put in a truck and taken to a wildlife park. As soon as he was released into the park, he immediately ran toward a giant tortoise. The frightened hippo tried to hide behind the huge creature. The 130-year-old tortoise, named Mzee, moved away. But Owen did not give up. He followed Mzee. Park officials think he was probably looking for help and safety. After a while, Mzee allowed Owen to come closer to him. Mzee started to act like a parent. If someone came too close to Owen, Mzee would try to chase the person away.

5   Now Mzee and Owen are seen together frequently. Owen stays near Mzee, and follows the tortoise closely around the park. They even sleep next to each other. Owen rests his head on the giant tortoise. He spends most of the day in the mud pond with the tortoise.

6   As Owen gets older, and bigger, wildlife park officials have to consider plans for his future. Owen cannot go back to a group of wild hippos. Male hippos might kill him to stop him from finding a female hippo. At some point, they plan to move Owen in with a 12-year-old female hippo in the park and hope that eventually the two will have a family.

Owen and Mzee

Checking Fluency and Comprehension

A. **Answer the questions. Do not look back at the text.**

1. What is true about Owen and Mzee?
   a. They are the same age.
   b. They are the same kind of animal.
   c. They are friends.

2. What happened to the baby hippo after the tsunami?
   a. He became separated from other animals in a wildlife park.
   b. He became separated from his family.
   c. He was washed back up the river.

3. Who rescued the baby hippo from the ocean?
   a. One person called Owen.
   b. A group of people on the beach.
   c. Officials in a wildlife park.

4. What did the tortoise do when it first met Owen?
   a. The tortoise moved away.
   b. The tortoise moved toward Owen.
   c. The tortoise tried to hide behind Owen.

5. Will Owen ever go back to the wild?
   a. Yes.
   b. No.
   c. Maybe.

B. **Check your answers with a partner. Record your score on page 169.**

Expanding Vocabulary

A. **Find the adverb forms of these adjectives in the text.**

1. sudden (par. 2) ....
2. immediate (par. 4) ....
3. probable (par. 4) ....
4. frequent (par. 5) ....
5. close (par. 5) ....
6. eventual (par. 6) ....

B. Fill in the blanks with the correct form of the words in italics.

1. The _____ storm made the roads unsafe for driving. (*sudden*)

2. We must leave _____ or we will miss our flight. (*immediate*)

3. You should _____ take an umbrella or you might get wet. (*probable*)

4. It is Mika's favorite coffee shop, so she is a _____ customer. (*frequent*)

5. Don't stand so _____ to the edge of that cliff. (*close*)

6. They are happy where they live now, but _____ they would like to move into a bigger house. (*eventual*)

What's Your Opinion?

A. What do you look for in a friend? Check (✔) your answers.

Someone who...	Very Important	Fairly Important	Not Important
1. is close in age	☐	☐	☐
2. is loyal	☐	☐	☐
3. is understanding	☐	☐	☐
4. has the same interests	☐	☐	☐
5. looks after me	☐	☐	☐

B. Discuss your answers with a partner. Give reasons for your answers.

Increasing Fluency

Scan the line to find the word on the left. Words may appear more than once. Can you finish in 15 seconds?

	a	b	c	d	e
1. river	liver	river	rival	river	risen
2. kill	kill	kills	sill	hill	gill
3. pond	bond	punt	pod	pond	pond
4. male	mail	mate	male	mare	hale
5. using	using	suing	doing	using	swing
6. drag	brag	drag	crag	pray	drag
7. saved	sawed	raved	saved	saves	caved
8. giant	giant	grant	giant	gaunt	gland

Extensive Reading 7

The Wizard of Oz

Introduction

This extract from an Oxford *Bookworms* reader gives you the opportunity to read more in English. The more you read, the faster and more fluent you will become. *The Wizard of Oz* is set in Kansas, USA, and a strange place far away. The story is about a girl named Dorothy who lives with her aunt and uncle and her dog, Toto, in Kansas. One day there is a strong wind storm called a tornado. The tornado blows Dorothy's house to a place far away. The extract you will read starts as the tornado lifts the house into the sky.

Before Reading

A. What do you think will happen in the extract? Check (✔) your answers.

...... 1. Dorothy's house lands in another town in the USA.

...... 2. Dorothy's house lands in a strange country with witches.

...... 3. Dorothy's house lands in the middle of the ocean.

...... 4. Dorothy's house lands in Europe.

B. Now read the extract to find out what happened.

Words

 CD 2 Track 4

The house moved, and then it went slowly up, up, up into the sky. Aunt Em and Uncle Henry were down in the cellar under the ground, but the house, Dorothy, and Toto went up to the top of the tornado. Dorothy looked through the open cellar door and saw hills and houses, a long way   50
down. She closed the cellar door quickly.

The wind blew the house along for many hours. At first Dorothy was afraid.

"But we can't do anything about it," she said to Toto. "So let's wait and see." And after two or three hours, she   100
and Toto went to sleep.

When Dorothy opened her eyes again, the house was on the ground, and everything was quiet. She picked up

Toto, opened the door, and went out. They saw tall trees, beautiful flowers, and little houses with blue doors.

Dorothy gave a little cry. "This isn't Kansas, Toto! And who are these people?"

There were three very short men in blue hats, coats and trousers, and a little old woman in a beautiful white dress. The woman walked up to Dorothy and said, "Thank you, thank you! Now the people are free!"

"Why are you thanking me?" Dorothy asked.

"You killed the Witch of the East," said the woman. "She was a bad witch, and her people, the Munchkins, were very afraid of her. Now she is dead, and we and the Munchkins want to thank you."

The little old woman and the three little men all smiled happily at Dorothy, but Dorothy did not understand.

"But I didn't kill anybody!" she said.

"Your house fell on the Witch," laughed the little woman. "Look! You can see her feet!"

Dorothy looked and saw two feet with red shoes under the house. Suddenly, one of the Munchkins gave a shout. "Look! Her feet are disappearing in the hot sun."

A second later, there were only the red shoes.

"Good," said the little woman. She picked up the shoes and gave them to Dorothy. "They're your shoes now. You must wear them because a witch's shoes can sometimes do wonderful things."

"Thank you," said Dorothy. "But who are you? Are you a Munchkin?"

"No, but I'm their friend. I'm the Witch of the North, and I came to see the dead Witch of the East. But don't be afraid—I'm a good witch."

"But Aunt Em says there aren't any witches."

400

"Oh yes, there are!" said the Witch. "Here in the country of Oz we have four witches. The witches of the North and the South are good witches, but those of the East and the West are bad witches. Now the Witch of the East is dead, so there is only one bad witch. We have a

450

famous wizard, too. We call him the Wizard of Oz, and he lives in the Emerald City. How many witches and wizards do you have in your country?"

"We don't have any," said Dorothy. Suddenly she remembered Aunt Em and Uncle Henry. "How can I get

500

back home to Kansas?" she asked.

350

"Where is Kansas?" asked the good Witch. "I don't know a country called Kansas, so I can't tell you the way."

Dorothy began to cry. "Oh, dear! What can I do?"

550 "Please don't cry!" said the Witch. "Go and see the Wizard of Oz. He's a good wizard, and perhaps he can help you. It's a long way, and you have to walk there. I can't go with you, but I can give you my kiss."

600 She gave Dorothy a little kiss. It looked like a small red flower on Dorothy's face.

"Now nothing can hurt you," she said. "Look—there is the road to the Emerald City. It is made of yellow bricks, so you can't lose your way…Goodbye."

"Goodbye!" said the three little Munchkins.

650 In the house Dorothy found some bread and some apples, and she put them all in a bag. Then she put on her blue and white dress. "Now I look nice," she said. She looked down at her old shoes. Then she remembered the bad Witch's red shoes and put them on.

700 She picked up her bag of food. "Come on, Toto!" she
Total Words: 710 called. "We're going to find the Wizard of Oz."

Extract from _The Wizard of Oz_, Bookworms Library, Oxford University Press.

After Reading

Answer the questions.

1. Who did the house fall on?

   ....

2. Who are the two good witches?

   ....

3. What did Dorothy do with the red shoes?

   ....

4. Where does the Wizard of Oz live?

   ....

Thinking About the Story

Answer the questions.

1. Did you enjoy reading the extract? Do you want to read more about Dorothy, her friends, and the Wizard?
2. Do you think Oz sounds like an interesting place?
3. Do you think Dorothy and Toto will be able to go home to Kansas?

Timed Repeated Reading

How many words can you read in one minute? Follow the instructions to practice increasing your reading speed.

1. Time yourself. Read the extract for one minute. When you stop, underline the last word you read and write "first" in the margin.
2. Go back to the beginning of the extract. Read again for one minute. Try to read faster this time. When you stop, underline the last word you read and write "second" in the margin.
3. Go back to the beginning of the extract. Read again for one minute. Try to read even faster this time. When you stop, underline the last word you read and write "third" in the margin.
4. Count the number of words you read each time. Record the three numbers on the Timed Repeated Reading Chart on page 169.

Looking Good

Discuss the questions.

1. Which person in the photograph do you think is most attractive?
2. Which person do you think is least attractive?

This unit is about what "looking good" means to people. In Part 1 you will read about one idea of beauty. In Part 2 you will read letters in a magazine advice column. The unit is followed by Extensive Reading 8, which is an extract from a book called *The Elephant Man*. It is about a man who has a difficult life because of the way he looks.

The Thin Line Between Beauty and Health

Before Reading

Read these opinions. Check (✔) any you agree with.

...... **1.** You have to be thin to be beautiful.

...... **2.** Being very thin is unhealthy.

...... **3.** Plump women are beautiful.

Comprehension Strategy: Recognizing Points of View

A point of view is an opinion. In some texts, the writer expresses his or her own opinion. In others, the writer summarizes other people's points of view instead. Look for words like *according to*, *says*, *believes*, and *thinks*.

A. **Read the text. Use the strategy to match the people with the opinions 1–3 above. There is one extra person.**

...... **a.** doctors

...... **b.** the author of the article

...... **c.** people who make advertisements

...... **d.** people in some African cultures

B. **Read the text again and answer the questions that follow.**

> 🎧 *CD 2 Track 5*
>
> ## The Thin Line Between Beauty and Health
>
> 1   They look nothing like ordinary people, and yet their images are everywhere. "They" are fashion models. They are on the covers of magazines and on TV. They are on advertising posters and in newspapers. They may be selling anything from cell phones to cosmetics. However, they are also selling something else. They are selling one particular idea of beauty, the idea that "to be thin is to be beautiful".
>
> 2   In the West, female models are now thinner than ever before. In the United States, fashion models now weigh 23 percent less than the average woman. Twenty years ago, this figure was just eight percent. In Asia, too, there is a trend toward thin models. One newspaper looked at the winners of a Korean beauty contest since 1975. It found that each year, the winner was taller and thinner than the year before. This idea of beauty is a big change from the past.

Until the 1970s in Korea, plump women were seen as healthy and attractive.

3   The idea that thin is beautiful used to be mainly connected with wealthy, Western societies. In the last 50 years, the international media has spread this idea around the world. From New York to Tokyo, magazines and advertisements show photos of thin models. These images seem to be having a big impact on how women see themselves. One recent survey looked at women from 10 different countries. They included Brazil, Argentina, Japan, and the United States. A third of the women were not happy with their weight. Even women of a healthy weight wanted to be thinner. In 1994, a study found that 90 percent of Korean high school girls of normal weight thought they were too fat.

4   Many women of normal weight are on diets to be thinner. Doctors worry that they are harming their health. They say people who diet a lot are more likely to have poor health and be depressed. The look that they are aiming for is unhealthy. Photos in magazines are often altered to make the models look even thinner than they are. No one in real life—not even the models—can look like the magazine images.

5   Not all cultures think thin is beautiful. In many African countries, people traditionally see plump women as beautiful. In some parts of Nigeria, women go to special houses before they get married. There, they eat more to put on weight for their wedding day. But how long will it be before even in these areas, women start wanting to be thin?

Checking Comprehension

A. **Complete the sentences.**

1. In the last 50 years, ...
   - a. Western societies have changed their idea of beauty.
   - b. a growing number of cultures see plump women as beautiful.
   - c. a growing number of cultures share the same idea about beauty.

2. Twenty years ago, fashion models in the United States ....
   - a. weighed the same amount as the average woman.
   - b. weren't as thin as they are today.
   - c. weighed the same amount as they do today.

3. Many women of normal weight go on diets to lose weight ....
   - a. because they are influenced by pictures in the media.
   - b. because they want to become models.
   - c. for health reasons.

4. Doctors say that going on diets to lose weight ....
   - a. is healthy.
   - b. is unhealthy.
   - c. is unhealthy for people who are normal weight.

5. Many photos in magazines ....
   - a. show what normal women really look like.
   - b. show what models really look like.
   - c. don't show what models really look like.

6. Cultures that see plump women as beautiful include ....
   - a. some parts of Nigeria.
   - b. Western countries.
   - c. Brazil.

Looking at Vocabulary in Context

A. Find the words in bold in the text. For each line, circle the word that does not belong.

1. **images** (par. 1)	pictures	photos	ideas
2. **cosmetics** (par. 1)	makeup	clothes	toiletries
3. **particular** (par. 1)	specific	exact	general
4. **plump** (par. 2)	slim	fat	heavy
5. **depressed** (par. 4)	unhappy	happy	sad
6. **altered** (par. 4)	changed	affected	unchanged

B. Fill in the blanks with the words in bold from A. Be sure to use the correct forms.

1. I don't watch movies with sad endings because they make me feel ....

2. The .... on flat screen TVs are clearer than on older TVs.

3. The police say the man tried to .... his appearance by dying his hair.

4. I won't use .... that have been tested on animals.

5. When I was a child I was quite .... , but my brother was really thin.

6. I like most of Paul Auster's novels, but I didn't enjoy that .... one.

What's Your Opinion?

A. Do you agree or disagree with the statements? Check (✔)your answers.

	Agree	Disagree	Not Sure
1. I think images in the media have some effect on me.	☐	☐	☐
2. I don't think images in the media have any effect on me.	☐	☐	☐
3. I think it's OK for advertisements to use pictures of thin models.	☐	☐	☐
4. I think more advertisements should use pictures of normal women.	☐	☐	☐
5. I know lots of people who are on diets to lose weight.	☐	☐	☐

B. Discuss your answers with a partner. Give reasons for your answers.

Before Reading

Which of these things is most important in a partner? Number them from 1 (most important) to 4 (least important).

...... good looks   ...... an outgoing personality

...... a sense of humor   ...... being a good listener

Fluency Strategy: Scanning

> Scanning is searching very fast for specific information—a fact, a number, a word, a phrase. Make a clear picture in your mind of the information you are looking for. Move your eyes quickly across the text. Don't read every word. When you find the information, stop and read the sentence.

A. **Read the statements and guess whether they are made by Jon (J) or Ms. Hope (H). Then scan the text to check.**

...... **1.** I need your help.

...... **2.** Lots of people don't care about movie star looks.

...... **3.** Girls like boys who are confident and good-looking.

...... **4.** It's important to be a good listener.

B. **Read the whole text quickly. Record your reading time below and in the chart on page 169.**

Start: _____
Finish: _____
Reading Time: _____

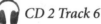 *CD 2 Track 6*

Just Ask!

Ms. Hope answers all of your questions on life and love.

Dear Ms. Hope,

1   I am a 19-year-old university student, and I need your help. I have been going out with my girlfriend for two months. We have a great relationship. We share the same sense of humor and have a lot in common. She seems to like me, and I'm crazy about her. There is only one problem. She thinks it is strange that I still haven't introduced her to my best friend.

2   The trouble is, I am worried that when she meets him, she will like him better than me. I know it sounds ridiculous, but all the girls try to catch his eye. He is tall and very good-looking. People say he looks like a movie star. He's also funny and much more outgoing than I am. I know he would never try to steal my girlfriend or anything, I'm just worried that she'll prefer him, and she'll lose interest in me.

3   I'm not very good-looking. For one thing, my skin hasn't been too good recently, so I don't feel very confident about my appearance. Also, I'm pretty short, and I wear glasses. I'm quite shy and quiet in social situations. In the past, when my friend and I have been out together, he is the one who does all the talking. Girls like boys who are confident and good-looking, so they all really like him.

4   I don't know what to do. I really like this girl, and I don't want her to break up with me. Can you help?

    — Jon

* * * * *

Dear Jon,

5   It sounds like you and your girlfriend are made for each other. What you need is some self-confidence. You say this girl likes you and that you have a good relationship. She is obviously happy with you the way you are. Lots of people don't care about movie star looks. Not everyone agrees on the definition of what makes a man good-looking. Some people prefer short men. And by the way, what's wrong with glasses? Many people say glasses make you look intelligent.

6   In any case, looks certainly aren't everything. I'm sure there are many things about you that your girlfriend finds attractive. She might like the fact that you are shy. Not everyone wants someone who talks all the time. It's important to be a good listener to others—it sounds like you're good at that.

7   It's time to introduce your friend and girlfriend. So go ahead. Get in touch with your friend and plan a meeting. Who knows, your girlfriend may like you even more after she meets your talkative friend!

    — Ms. Hope

Checking Fluency and Comprehension

A. Complete the sentences. Do not look back at the text.

1. Jon wrote the letter because ....
   a. he wants advice.
   b. he wants to meet Ms. Hope.

2. Jon is not very happy about his ....
   a. relationship with his girlfriend.
   b. appearance.

3. Jon's girlfriend ....
   a. has never met Jon's friend.
   b. likes tall men better than short men.

4. Ms. Hope tells Jon he should ....
   a. change his appearance.
   b. introduce his friend and girlfriend.

5. Ms. Hope thinks Jon should be more ....
   a. self-confident.
   b. talkative and outgoing.

B. Check your answers with a partner. Record your score on page 169.

Expanding Vocabulary

A. When certain words are used together in a phrase, they take on a new meaning. These phrases are called idioms. Find the idioms in bold in the text. Then match the halves of the definitions.

.... 1. If you are **going out** with someone (par. 1),

a. you contact them by phone or email.

.... 2. If you are **crazy about** someone (par. 1),

b. you love them very much.

.... 3. If you **catch** someone's **eye** (par. 2),

c. you attract someone's attention.

.... 4. If you **break up** with someone (par. 4),

d. you are a well-matched couple.

.... 5. If you are **made for** each other (par. 5),

e. you stop having a relationship with them.

.... 6. If you **get in touch** with someone (par. 7),

f. you have a relationship with them as girlfriend or boyfriend.

B. Fill in the blanks with the words in bold from A. Use the correct forms.

The first time I saw Tom, he was waiting at the bus stop. He (1) _____ caught _____ my
_____ eye _____ because he looked so happy. I asked him the time, we started chatting,
and after a while we exchanged phone numbers. He (2) _____ with me the
next day, and we arranged to meet. Soon we started (3) _____ with each
other. I was completely in love with him, and he said he was (4) _____ me.
All my friends said we were (5) _____ each other. One day he told me he
wanted to ask me something important. For some reason I was suddenly scared he
was going to (6) _____ with me, but he asked me to marry him!

What's Your Opinion?

A. Do you agree or disagree with the statements? Check (✔) your answers.

	Agree	Disagree	Not Sure
1. I don't think Jon should worry so much about his looks.	☐	☐	☐
2. I think Jon should try wearing contact lenses instead of glasses.	☐	☐	☐
3. I think Jon should try to be more talkative.	☐	☐	☐
4. I think Jon should talk to his girlfriend about his feelings.	☐	☐	☐
5. I think Ms. Hope gave good advice to Jon.	☐	☐	☐

B. Discuss your answers with a partner. Give reasons for your answers.

Increasing Fluency

Scan the line to find the word on the left. Words may appear more than once. Can you
finish in 15 seconds?

	a	b	c	d	e
1. funny	sunny	bunny	(funny)	furry	fussy
2. short	short	snort	sharp	short	start
3. share	snare	share	stare	flare	scare
4. shy	sty	sly	shy	cry	shy
5. meets	meats	meet	teams	meets	seem
6. lose	lose	loose	loss	rose	close
7. fact	act	fact	pact	fast	fact
8. other	mother	otter	other	offer	outer

Extensive Reading 8

The Elephant Man

Introduction

This extract from an Oxford *Bookworms* reader gives you the opportunity to read more in English. The more you read, the faster and more fluent you will become. *The Elephant Man* is set in London, England, in 1884. It is a true story about a poor, very ugly man named Joseph Merrick. People pay money to look at him like an animal at the zoo. One day, a doctor named Frederick Treves pays money to see Merrick. He wants to take him to the hospital to study him. The extract you will read starts when Dr. Treves picks Merrick up to take him to the hospital.

Before Reading

A. What do you think will happen in the extract? Check (✔) your answers.

...... **1.** Boys laugh at Merrick because he looks strange.

...... **2.** Dr. Treves does surgery on Merrick to make him look better.

...... **3.** Merrick refuses to go to the hospital.

...... **4.** Dr. Treves examines Merrick carefully at the hospital.

B. Now read the extract to see what happens.

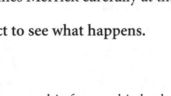 *CD 2 Track 7*

Words

I could not see his face or his body. He had an enormous black hat on his head, like a big box. A grey cloth came down from the hat, in front of his face. There was a hole in the cloth in front of his eyes. He could see out of the   50
hole but I could not see in. He wore a long black coat, too. The coat began at his neck, and ended at his feet, so I could not see his arms, his body, or his legs. On his feet he wore big shoes, like old bags.   100

He had a stick in his left hand, and he walked very slowly. I opened the door of the cab, and got out.

"Good morning, Mr. Merrick," I said. "Can you get in?"

"Elpmyupasteps," he said.

"I'm sorry," I said. "I don't understand."

For a minute he stood by the door of the cab and said nothing. Then he hit the cab with his stick.

"STEPS!" he said loudly. "Help me up the steps!"

Then I understood. There were three steps up into the cab, and he could not get up them.

"Yes, I see. I'm sorry," I said. "Let me help you."

I took his left hand and began to help him. My right hand was behind his back. I felt very strange. His left hand was like a young woman's, but his back, under the coat, was horrible. I could feel the bags of old skin on his back under the coat.

He put one enormous foot on the first step, and then he stopped. After a minute, he moved his second foot slowly. Then he stopped and waited again.

"Hello, sir. Can I help you?"

I looked behind me. It was the postman. And behind him, I could see three young boys. One of the boys laughed.

The postman smiled. "Is the gentleman sick?" he asked.

I thought quickly. "Yes. But this is a lady, not a gentleman. I'm a doctor, and she's ill. Take her hand, so I can help her better."

The postman took Merrick's left hand, and I helped him with two hands from behind. Slowly, very slowly, Merrick went up the steps and into the cab.

One boy was very near the cab. He called to his friends.

"Come and see this, boys! A fat lady in a black coat! And look at that enormous hat!"

The boys laughed. They were very near the cab too, now. I closed the door quickly.

"Thank you," I said to the postman.

"That's all right, sir," he said. "She's a strange lady, sir, isn't she?"

"She's sick, that's all," I said quickly. "We're going to the hospital. Goodbye, and thank you."

The cab drove down the road to the hospital. I looked at Merrick. "That was difficult, wasn't it?" I said.

At first he said nothing, but then he spoke. His voice was very strange, but I listened to him carefully, and I could understand him.

"The steps were very difficult," he said. "But most things are difficult for me."

"Yes," I said. "Nothing is easy for you, is it?"

"No," he said. He was very quiet for a minute. Then he said, "Who are you, sir?"

"Who am I? Oh, I'm sorry. My name is Dr. Treves. Here, this is my card."

300

350

400

450

500

550

I gave him a card with my name on. Then I thought, "That was no good. This man can't read." But Merrick took the card and looked at it very carefully. Then he put it in his pocket.

Dr. Frederick Treves

The London Hospital,
Whitechapel,
London, E1.

600

650

Total Words: 670

I did not talk to him very much at the hospital. I looked at his head and arms and legs and body very carefully. Then I wrote the important things about him in a little book. A nurse helped me. Merrick looked at her sometimes, but she did not smile at him or talk to him. I think she was afraid of him. I think Merrick was afraid too, because he was very quiet.

Extract from *The Elephant Man*, Bookworms Library, Oxford University Press.

After Reading

Answer the questions.

1. What was Merrick wearing?

   ....

2. What did Merrick ask Dr. Treves to do?

   ....

3. What did Dr. Treves give Merrick in the cab?

   ....

4. What happened at the hospital?

   ....

Thinking About the Story

Answer the questions.

1. Did you enjoy reading the extract? Do you want to read more about Merrick and Dr. Treves?
2. Have you ever laughed at someone because they looked very different?
3. Do you think Dr. Treves will help Merrick?

Timed Repeated Reading

How many words can you read in one minute? Follow the instructions to practice increasing your reading speed.

1. Time yourself. Read the extract for one minute. When you stop, underline the last word you read and write "first" in the margin.
2. Go back to the beginning of the extract. Read again for one minute. Try to read faster this time. When you stop, underline the last word you read and write "second" in the margin.
3. Go back to the beginning of the extract. Read again for one minute. Try to read even faster this time. When you stop, underline the last word you read and write "third" in the margin.
4. Count the number of words you read each time. Record the three numbers on the Timed Repeated Reading Chart on page 169.

Unit 9

Personality

Discuss the questions.

1. Is your personality similar to either of your parents'?
2. Do you think you are generally a happy person?

This unit is about what makes us the way we are. In Part 1, you will read about what makes people's personalities different from one another. In Part 2, you will read about what makes people happy. The unit is followed by Extensive Reading 9, which is an extract from a book called *Aladdin and the Enchanted Lamp*. It is about a boy and his uncle, whose personality may not be what it seems.

Before Reading

Look up the meaning of the words you do not know. Circle the ones that best describe your personality.

rebellious	active	quiet	reserved
unfriendly	fun-loving	responsible	dependable

Comprehension Strategy: Recognizing Reference Words

> We use reference words instead of repeating the names of people, places, ideas, or other things. Look out for common reference words like *it, them, this, that*, etc. Look at sentences nearby to find what they refer to. They, can refer to one word or a group of words.

A. Read the text. Use the strategy to find what these words refer to.

1. their (par. 5) ....

2. it (par. 6) ....

3. others (par. 6) ....

4. one of these (par. 7) ....

5. this (par. 8) ....

B. Read the text again and answer the questions that follow.

🎧 *CD 2 Track 8*

Understanding Ourselves

1   Fei, Meilan, and Lihua Lin are sisters. They live in the same city, and they are studying to be doctors at the same university. But they are very different in their behavior and personality.

2   Fei is friendly and outgoing; she likes to be around other people. Fei is rebellious. She doesn't like to follow rules, and she likes to do things her own way. She is very active, and she enjoys going to restaurants, parties, and music concerts.

3   Meilan is a happy person, but, unlike Fei, she prefers to be alone. She has two good friends whom she sees two or three times a month. Meilan likes structure, and she doesn't like change. She is happiest when she stays at home and reads a book or watches a movie.

4   Lihua is quiet and reserved. She doesn't smile or laugh very often. Some people who don't know her very well think she is unfriendly. But her best friend says she can depend on Lihua and that other people just don't understand her.

5   What makes their personalities so different? There are many theories about where personality and behavior come from.

6   Most scientists agree that our personalities are influenced by both our genes and our environment. However, there is much debate about which of these is the most important. Some scientists believe that a person's personality is mainly inherited. The idea is that genes from our parents make us the way we are. This suggests that our personality is decided by nature, so we cannot easily change it. Others say that our environment is the most important influence on our personality and behavior. As we grow up, our personalities are influenced by our surroundings and the way our parents raise us. This is often called the "nurture" theory.

7   There are many other popular theories about what makes us the way we are. One of these is that personality is defined by blood type—A, B, O, or AB. People with type A blood like to follow rules. People with type O blood are the opposite—they dislike rules and structure.

8   Other people think our position in the family, compared with our brothers and sisters, is important. They point to whether we are the oldest or youngest child, for example. They say that this has a big influence on our personalities as adults. For example, they say the youngest child often grows up to be fun-loving and rebellious. The oldest child is more likely to be responsible and dependable.

9   Fei, Meilan, and Lihua don't know what makes each of them the way they are. Perhaps the most important thing is that they get along with each other despite their differences.

Checking Comprehension

Answer the questions.

1. What is the main idea of this article?
   a. Fei, Meilan, and Lihua don't know what makes each of them the way they are.
   b. Our personalities are influenced by our genes and the way we grew up.
   c. There are many explanations about what makes people's personalities different.

2. In what way are Fei, Meilan, and Lihua similar?
   a. their personality
   b. their position in the family compared with their brothers and sisters
   c. the environment in which they grew up

3. According to the nurture theory, what is the most important influence on our personalities?
   a. our blood type
   b. the environment in which we grow up
   c. genes from our parents

4. Which factors do scientists believe can explain our personalities?
   a. genes from our parents and our environment when we were young
   b. genes from our parents and our blood type
   c. our environment when we were young and our blood type

5. What might people who believe the blood type theory say about Meilan?
   a. Meilan's blood type is probably type A.
   b. Meilan's blood type is probably type O.
   c. Meilan is probably the oldest sister.

6. What might people who believe the family order theory say about Fei?
   a. Fei's blood type is probably type O.
   b. Fei is probably the oldest sister.
   c. Fei is probably the youngest sister.

Looking at Vocabulary

A. Find the words in bold in the text. Circle the word or phrase with the closest meaning.

1. **outgoing** (par. 2)
   a. likes to be with people   **b.** enjoys music

2. **rebellious** (par. 2)
   a. unfriendly   **b.** not willing to follow rules

3. **reserved** (par. 4)
   a. talkative   **b.** shy

4. **environment** (par. 6)
   a. human biology   **b.** surroundings

5. **inherited** (par. 6)
   a. present at birth   **b.** formed while growing up

6. **dependable** (par. 8)
   a. reliable   **b.** can't be trusted

B. Fill in the blanks with the words in bold from A.

1. People say that building a new airport will damage the _____.

2. I often got into trouble with my teachers because I was so _____.

3. You need to be very _____ to become a sales representative, because you meet new people all the time.

4. My boss is very _____ so she hates giving speeches.

5. People say I _____ my looks from my mother.

6. It's strange that Max is late because he's usually so _____.

What's Your Opinion?

A. What effect do you think these things have on your personality? Check (✔) your answers.

	Big Effect	Some Effect	No Effect
1. The environment you grew up in	☐	☐	☐
2. Your position in the family (oldest/youngest/middle child)	☐	☐	☐
3. Your blood type	☐	☐	☐
4. Your genes	☐	☐	☐
5. The month you were born in	☐	☐	☐

B. Discuss your answers with a partner. Give reasons for your answers.

Part 2 Happy People

Before Reading

Which of these things would make you happy? Number them from 1 (most important) to 6 (least important).

...... winning the lottery   ...... doing hobbies you enjoy

...... having lots of friends   ...... having good health

...... having a successful career   ...... having nice things

Fluency Strategy: Skimming for the Main Idea

Skimming is reading fast to understand the writer's main idea, or message. Read the title, the first paragraph, and the first sentences in the other paragraphs. Then read the last paragraph. Read quickly; details are not important.

A. **Use the strategy to skim the text. Circle the main idea.**

   1. Some people are happy and others are unhappy.

   2. It is difficult to be happy.

   3. The things that make us happy are often not the things we expect.

B. **Read the whole text quickly. Record your reading time below and in the chart on page 169.**

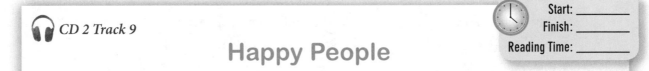

🎧 *CD 2 Track 9*

Start: _____
Finish: _____
Reading Time: _____

Happy People

1   Why do some people seem to be happier than others? Researchers interviewed thousands of people to try to find the answer. They discovered that what makes us happy is often not what we expect.

2   One important factor, say the researchers, is people's attitude toward life. Many people seem to be happy with their lives even when they don't seem to have very much to be happy about. People with a positive attitude may still be happy even after bad events. In contrast, many people who seem to have all the good things in life—health, money, family—are still unhappy. Someone who has a negative attitude toward life may still be unhappy even if good things happen to them. For example, one study found that lottery winners don't end up any happier than other people.

3   Another factor is the activities we do. Happy people spend most of their time doing satisfying activities. People are most satisfied when they do work or hobbies they enjoy and feel they are good at. This doesn't mean people have to be very successful by society's standards. For example, a successful company director may not be happy. She might secretly wish she could just work on her garden all day.

4   Unhappy people are more likely to judge themselves against other people, say researchers. People who are not happy feel that they don't have enough of the good things in life. In contrast, happy people don't judge themselves by what other people have. Happy people set their own goals. They decide what they think is important in life.

5   A further factor is the time we spend with other people. The researchers found that happy people are sociable people. They spend a lot of their time with other people in social situations. They live a busy and full social life. They spend time with people at work, in school, in clubs, with their friends and family members. In contrast, people who spend a lot of time alone are more likely to be unhappy.

6   A good relationship with a partner is also an important factor. The better that relationship is, the happier a person is.

7   The research shows many of us are not good at predicting what will make us happy. We might think that winning the lottery is the answer. In fact, the real answer lies closer to home—in our own attitude, our friends and family, and our everyday activities.

Checking Fluency and Comprehension

A. Answer the questions. Do not look back at the text.

1. According to the researchers, what has the biggest influence on happiness?
   a. Money.
   b. Health.
   c. Attitude.

2. According to the researchers, who is likely to be happier?
   a. People who are active.
   b. People who don't have much to do.
   c. Neither of the above.

3. Why does the text mention a successful company director?
   a. To give an example of a happy, active person.
   b. To show that success at work doesn't always make you happy.
   c. To give an example of someone doing a hobby they enjoy.

4. According to the researchers, who is likely to be happier?
   a. People who spend time with friends.
   b. People who spend time alone.
   c. Neither of the above.

5. Why does the text mention winning the lottery?
   a. To show winning the lottery makes people happy.
   b. To show winning the lottery makes people unhappy.
   c. To show winning the lottery doesn't have much affect on happiness.

B. Check your answers with a partner. Record your score on page 169.

Expanding Vocabulary

A. Find the verb forms of these nouns in the text.

1. expectation (par. 1) ....
2. satisfaction (par. 3) ....
3. enjoyment (par. 3) ....
4. judgment (par. 4) ....
5. decision (par. 4) ....
6. prediction (par. 7) ....

B. Fill in the blanks with the correct form of the words from A.

1. I hope you don't regret your _____ to go to a school that is so far from home.

2. Are you _____ with your job, or are you looking for a career change?

3. I'm not psychic, but many of the _____ I've made have come true.

4. Alice did not _____ any visitors, so she turned out the lights and went to bed.

5. Joe really _____ watching the baseball game with his friend yesterday.

6. You shouldn't make any harsh _____ about your new teacher before you've met her.

What's Your Opinion?

A. How often do you do these things? Check (✔) your answers.

	Often	Sometimes	Not Often
1. I spend time doing things I enjoy.	☐	☐	☐
2. I spend time doing things I don't really enjoy.	☐	☐	☐
3. I spend time with friends.	☐	☐	☐
4. I spend time on my own.	☐	☐	☐
5. I think about winning the lottery.	☐	☐	☐

B. Discuss your answers with a partner. Give reasons for your answers.

Increasing Fluency

Scan the line to find the word on the left. Words may appear more than once. Can you finish in 15 seconds?

	a	b	c	d	e
1. full	fill	full	fall	fell	full
2. happy	nappy	happy	happy	sappy	pappy
3. spend	spend	spent	spell	spurn	spend
4. than	thin	then	than	them	than
5. time	time	time	dime	lime	tine
6. work	work	word	worm	wok	work
7. still	sill	spill	still	sill	skill
8. health	health	heath	healed	health	stealth

Extensive Reading 9

Aladdin and the Enchanted Lamp

Introduction

This extract from an Oxford *Bookworms* reader gives you the opportunity to read more in English. The more you read, the faster and more fluent you will become. *Aladdin and the Enchanted Lamp* is set many years ago in a city in Arabia. The story is about a boy named Aladdin. Aladdin and his mother are very poor. One day Aladdin meets a man named Abanazar who says he is his uncle. Abanazar seems very friendly and says he wants to help them. The extract you will read begins with Abanazar asking Aladdin to go with him on a trip outside the city. Is Abanazar really as friendly as he seems?

Before Reading

A. What do you think will happen in the extract? Check (✔) your answers.

...... **1.** Abanazar and Aladdin become good friends.

...... **2.** Abanazar makes Aladdin find something for him.

...... **3.** Abanazar shuts Aladdin in a dark place in the ground.

...... **4.** Abanazar gives Aladdin something that will make him rich.

B. Now read the extract to see what happens.

🎧 *CD 2 Track 10*

Words

"You are very good to me, Uncle," Aladdin said.

Abanazar smiled. "But of course," he said. "You are my brother's son. Now, let us leave the city and go up into the hills. There is something wonderful there, and you must see it."

They left the gardens, walked past the Sultan's palace, and out of the city up into the hills. They walked for a long time, and Aladdin began to feel tired.   50

"It's not far now," said Abanazar. "We're going to see a beautiful garden—more beautiful than the garden of the Sultan's palace."

At last Abanazar stopped. "Here we are," he said.   100

Aladdin looked, but he could see no gardens on the hills. "Where is this garden, Uncle?" he said.

"First we must make a fire," said Abanazar.

Aladdin did not understand, but he made a fire for his uncle on the ground. Then Abanazar took some powder out of a small box, and put it on the fire. He closed his eyes and said, *"Abracadabra!"*

150

At once, the sky went dark. Black smoke came from the fire, and the ground under the fire began to open. Then the smoke went away, and in the ground there was now a big white stone with a ring in it.

200

Aladdin was very afraid. He began to run away, but Abanazar took his arm and hit him on the head.

For a minute or two Aladdin could not speak or move. Then he cried, "Why did you do that, Uncle?"

250

"You must be a man now, not a child," said Abanazar. "I am your father's brother, and you must obey me. Don't be afraid. In a short time you're going to be a rich man. Now, listen carefully." He took Aladdin's hand. "Only you can move this stone. Put your hand on the ring and say your name and your father's name."

Very afraid, Aladdin put his hand on the ring. It was not hot, but very cold. "I am Aladdin, son of Mustafa," he said. The stone moved easily, and now Aladdin could see stairs under the ground.

"Go down those stairs," Abanazar said, "and then through four big rooms. In the last room there is a door into a garden, and under one of the trees there is a lamp. You can take some fruit from the trees, but first you must find the lamp. Bring the lamp to me."

"Please come with me, Uncle!" Aladdin said.

"No. Only you can do this, my boy." Abanazar took a gold ring off his finger and gave it to Aladdin. "This ring is magic and can protect you," he said. "Be careful, and bring me the lamp quickly!"

Aladdin put the ring on the little finger of his left hand and began to go down the stairs. It was dark and he was afraid, but he was more afraid of Abanazar.

And Aladdin was right to be afraid, because Abanazar was not his uncle. He was a magician from Morocco, and he wanted this lamp very much. It was a magic lamp, and only a poor boy from the city could get it for him—a boy named Aladdin.

Aladdin went down a hundred stairs and into the first room. Down here, it was not dark and he went quickly through the rooms to the door into the garden. There were trees in the garden with beautiful fruit of different colors—white, red, green, and yellow.

He soon found the lamp, under one of the trees. "Why does my uncle want this dirty old lamp?" he thought. He put it in his pocket. Then he began to take fruit from the trees, and to put it in every pocket of his coat. After that he went back to

the stairs and began to go up. Soon he could see Abanazar and the blue sky.

"Give the lamp to me," Abanazar said, and put out his hand. "Quickly, boy, the lamp!"

Aladdin could not get the lamp out of his pocket because it was under the fruit. He looked at Abanazar's angry face and was afraid.

"First help me out, then you can have the lamp," he said. "Please, Uncle!"

"First the lamp," cried Abanazar. "Give me the lamp!"

"No!" Aladdin said.

"You good-for-nothing! You dog! You and the lamp can stay down there!" Angrily, Abanazar ran to the fire and put more powder on it. *"Abracadabra!"* he called.

The big white stone moved again, and now Aladdin could not see the sky. He was in the dark, under the ground, and could not get out.

Extract from *Aladdin and the Enchanted Lamp*, Bookworms Library, Oxford University Press.

650

700

750
Total Words: 765

After Reading

Answer the questions.

1. Who is Abanazar?

   ....

2. What did Abanazar put on the fire?

   ....

3. What did Aladdin see in the garden?

   ....

4. Did Aladdin give Abanazar the lamp?

   ....

Thinking About the Story

Answer the questions.

1. Did you enjoy reading the extract? Do you want to read more about Aladdin?
2. Do you like Abanazar? Why or why not?
3. Do you think Aladdin will get out of the cave?

Timed Repeated Reading

How many words can you read in one minute? Follow the instructions to practice increasing your reading speed.

1. Time yourself. Read the extract for one minute. When you stop, underline the last word you read and write "first" in the margin.
2. Go back to the beginning of the extract. Read again for one minute. Try to read faster this time. When you stop, underline the last word you read and write "second" in the margin.
3. Go back to the beginning of the extract. Read again for one minute. Try to read even faster this time. When you stop, underline the last word you read and write "third" in the margin.
4. Count the number of words you read each time. Record the three numbers on the Timed Repeated Reading Chart on page 169.

Unit 10

Animals

Discuss the questions.

1. What different ways can you think of that people use animals?

2. Which animals are especially important to people in your country?

This unit is about animals which are important to humans. In Part 1, you will read about how camels are helping people in Kenya. In Part 2, you will read about an animal which has a special place in an old story. The unit is followed by Extensive Reading 10, which is an extract from a book called *The Coldest Place on Earth*. It is about a race to the South Pole led by a group of brave men and working dogs.

Part 1   The Camel Library

Before Reading

Mark the statements true (T) or false (F).

.... **1.** Camels are found in the African country of Kenya.

.... **2.** Camels cannot walk easily on rough roads.

.... **3.** Camels can carry heavy loads.

.... **4.** Camels cannot travel long distances without water.

Comprehension Strategy: Identifying Meaning from Context

You can often work out the meaning of words you don't know from the words and phrases nearby. Try to work out the part of speech (noun, verb, adjective, adverb) of the new word. Look at the sentences before and after the word. They may use words with the same meaning, or with the opposite meaning.

A. **The words in bold have more than one meaning. Find the words in the text. Use the strategy to work out the meanings, then circle the answers.**

1. **Like** (par. 1) means *enjoy (v) / similar to (prep)*.

2. **Mobile** (par. 3) means *something that moves (adj) / a children's toy (n)*.

3. **Poor** (par. 3) means *not having enough money (adj) / to be in a bad condition (adj)*.

4. **Ground** (par. 5) means *a child stays home as punishment (v) / the earth (n)*.

B. **Read the text again and answer the questions that follow.**

🎧 *CD 2 Track 11*

The Camel Library

1   The camel library is like no other library. It is unique to Kenya. Like traditional libraries, books can be borrowed and returned. Unlike traditional libraries, the books are carried to people by camels.

2   The camel library was started in northern Kenya, where many people live in remote villages. Their nearest town, called Garissa, is hundreds of kilometers away. Many of the villagers have never learned to read. They cannot afford to

---

buy books, let alone have access to the Internet. Until 1996, the only library in the area was in Garissa. The distance meant villagers could not get to it.

3   The problem was solved with the creation of a mobile library. However, while mobile libraries in other places use trucks, this one uses camels to take the books to the villages. Camels are often the most efficient form of transportation in Northern Kenya, as the poor roads make driving difficult. Trucks, buses, and cars often break down. Camels can carry heavy things and travel long distances without water. And, unlike trucks, they don't need good roads.

4   The Camel Library uses three camels. They carry more than 200 books to ten villages in northern Kenya. Four people travel with the camels. One of them acts as a guard to make sure no one tries to steal the books—or the camels—along the way. The camels walk from one village to another, five days a week. The Camel Library spends one day in each village, and then goes to the next small town. It visits each village once every two weeks.

5   The Camel Library is very popular. At each of the ten villages, the children eagerly wait for the camels to come. The Camel Library is their only source of reading material. Everyone in the village helps unload the books from the camels. The books are spread out on the ground, under some big trees. At the end of the day, everyone helps load the books onto the camels and thinks about the next visit in two weeks.

6   The books are in English, which the children in the villages are learning as a foreign language in school. Swahili is the national language of Kenya, but there are not many books written in Swahili.

7   Books can be borrowed for only two weeks at a time. If someone finishes a book quickly, he or she will have to wait until the Camel Library comes again before getting another one.

Checking Comprehension

A. Mark the statements true (T) or false (F). Correct the ones which are false.

...... 1. The unique feature of the Camel Library is that it moves from place to place.

....

...... 2. No other libraries anywhere else in the world use camels.

....

...... 3. Camels are used because there aren't many trucks in northern Kenya.

....

...... 4. The Camel Library stays in each village for five days.

....

...... 5. The villagers don't have access to books from anywhere else.

....

...... 6. The books in the Camel Library are in Swahili, the national language.

....

B. Complete the chart with the missing information.

	Problem	Solution
1. Cost of books	Villagers don't have enough money to buy books.	Villagers can borrow books from a library instead of buying books.
2. Distance	....	Started a mobile library.
3. Transport	Roads are bad, so driving is difficult.	....
4. Risks	People might steal the books along the way.	....

130 Unit 10 Animals

Looking at Vocabulary in Context

A. **Find the words in bold in the text. Circle the odd word out in each line.**

1. **remote** (par. 2)	nearby	distant	far away
2. **efficient** (par. 3)	expensive	economical	effective
3. **break down** (par. 3)	stop working	start working	fail
4. **eagerly** (par. 5)	excitedly	happily	quietly
5. **material** (par. 5)	matter	things	transport
6. **unload** (par. 5)	unpack	take down	pack

B. **Fill in the blanks with the words in bold from A. Use the correct forms.**

1. It took hours to .... the car because we had so much luggage.

2. My cell phone doesn't work in .... areas like the mountains.

3. I was late for class yesterday because the bus ....

4. Hundreds of fans are waiting .... for Johnny Depp to arrive at the movie theater.

5. I take lecture notes on my laptop because it's more .... than taking notes by hand.

6. I got bored waiting at reception because the only reading .... they had was old magazines.

What's Your Opinion?

A. **Check (✔) the statements that are true for northern Kenya. Then check (✔) those that are true for your country.**

	Northern Kenya	Your Country
1. Most people can get books easily.	☐	☐
2. Most people have Internet access.	☐	☐
3. There are mobile libraries.	☐	☐
4. Camels are the most efficient form of transportation.	☐	☐
5. Children learn English in school.	☐	☐

B. **Discuss your answers with a partner. Which things are the same in your country and northern Kenya? Which things are different?**

Part 2 | A Living Legend?

Before Reading

Discuss the questions.

1. How long do turtles live?
2. Do you know what a legend is?

Fluency Strategy: Predicting the Topic

You can often predict the topic before you read. The topic is the general subject of the text. Look at the title and the pictures in the text. These will give you clues about the topic.

A. **Use the strategy to predict the topic. Then skim to check your answer.**

1. Protecting the environment for turtles.
2. A famous turtle living in Vietnam.
3. Legends from around the world.

B. **Read the whole text quickly. Record your reading time below and in the chart on page 169.**

🎧 *CD 2 Track 12*

Start: _____
Finish: _____
Reading Time: _____

A Living Legend?

1   Hoan Kiem Lake is an oasis of calm in the middle of the city of Hanoi. Local people and tourists don't just come here to escape from the noise of the city. They also hope to see the famous Hoan Kiem turtle.

2   The legend of the Hoan Kiem turtle is well known in Vietnam. The legend goes back to the fifteenth century, when China ruled the country. According to the story, the gods gave a magic sword to the Vietnamese ruler, Emperor Le Loi. They told him to use it to defeat the Chinese army. After he defeated the Chinese, Le Loi was in a boat on a beautiful lake. A giant turtle rose out of the water and told him to return the sword. Before the Emperor could speak, the sword flew out of his hand and into the turtle's mouth. The turtle then disappeared into the lake, and returned the sword to the gods. From that day on, the lake was known as the Ho Hoan Kiem, or the Lake of the Returned Sword.

The Hoan Kiem turtle

3   Some people think the legend of the turtle is just a story. However, some scientists say the lake really is home to a unique species of giant turtle. There have been many sightings of the turtles over the years. Three turtles were seen in the 1960s. Researchers say the turtles are around two meters long, and weigh about 200 kilograms.

4   Dr. Ha Dinh Duc, a professor at Hanoi National University, has studied the Hoan Kiem turtles since 1991. He believes one of these turtles is the turtle in the legend. This would make it at least 550 years old. The first time Dr. Duc saw one of the giant turtles was in 1991. Until then, he had believed the turtles had all died. He says it was love at first sight.

5   He believes there now may only be one giant turtle left in the lake. If so, then it may be the last of its kind in the world. Dr. Duc has searched elsewhere in Vietnam and China for more, but he has only been able to find bones.

6   Dr. Duc has promised to protect the turtle, which he calls "great grandfather." He believes the lake should remain a safe environment for the turtle. There is now a plan to clean up the lake, so that the turtle will survive in real life as well as in the legend.

Checking Fluency and Comprehension

A. Answer the questions. Do not look back at the text.

1. Why is the Hoan Kiem turtle famous?
    a. Because it is the biggest turtle in the world.
    b. Because it is thought to be the turtle in a famous legend.
    c. Because it lives in the middle of a city.

2. According to the legend, how did Emperor Le Loi get the magic sword?
    a. He was given it by the turtle.
    b. He found it in the middle of the lake.
    c. He was given it by the gods.

3. According to Dr. Ha Dinh Duc, how old is the turtle?
    a. Over 200 years old.
    b. Over 300 years old.
    c. Over 500 years old.

4. Who has the nickname "great grandfather"?
    a. The turtle.
    b. Dr. Ha Dinh Duc.
    c. Emporer Le Loi.

5. How does Dr. Ha Dinh Duc think the turtle should be protected?
    a. By not letting people get too close to the lake.
    b. By protecting the environment of the lake.
    c. By making the legend more well known.

B. Check your answers with a partner. Record your score on page 169.

Expanding Vocabulary

A. Find six nouns in the text which end in the suffixes *–ist*, *–er*, or *–or*. Complete the chart. Can you think of any more?

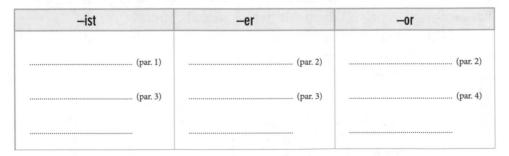

–ist	–er	–or
.... (par. 1)	.... (par. 2)	.... (par. 2)
.... (par. 3)	.... (par. 3)	.... (par. 4)
....	....	....

B. Use the nouns from A to complete the definitions.

1. A/An .... is someone who leads a country.

2. A/An .... is someone who leads an empire.

3. A/An .... is an expert in biology, chemistry, or physics.

4. A/An .... is a university teacher.

5. A/An .... is someone who studies a subject in detail.

6. A/An .... is someone who visits a place on vacation.

What's Your Opinion?

A. Answer the questions for yourself.

	You	Your Partner
1. Do you believe a turtle can live more than 500 years?	....	....
2. Do you think the legend could be true?	....	....
3. Do you think the Hoan Kiem turtle is the one in the legend?	....	....
4. Do you think the professor will be able to protect the turtle in the future?	....	....
5. Do you know any other legends about animals?	....	....

B. Ask a partner the same questions. Discuss your answers. Give reasons for your answers.

Increasing Fluency

Scan the line to find the word on the left. Words may appear more than once. Can you finish in 15 seconds?

	a	b	c	d	e
1. known	known	know	noun	knows	known
2. one	ore	one	one	owe	lone
3. story	store	stony	stop	story	story
4. last	last	lost	last	list	lest
5. weigh	weight	might	weigh	weigh	sleigh
6. safe	sale	safe	sage	safer	safe
7. plan	plan	plant	pram	pain	plan
8. bones	bone	bores	bones	tones	gone

Extensive Reading 10

The Coldest Place on Earth

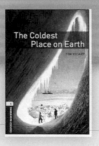

Introduction

This extract from an Oxford *Bookworms* reader gives you the opportunity to read more in English. The more you read, the faster and more fluent you will become. *The Coldest Place on Earth* is set in 1910. It is a true story about a Norwegian man named Roald Amundsen. He has gathered a team of men to go with him to the North Pole. It will be a long journey by sea—first sailing south around Cape Horn in South America, then north up to Alaska, then across ice, with skis and dogs, to the Arctic and the North Pole. But Amundsen has a change of plan which the other men don't yet know about. He wants to go to the South Pole, in Antarctica, instead. The extract you will read begins with Amundsen and his friends on the ship. They need to get the dogs that will help them cross the ice.

Before Reading

A. What do you think will happen in the extract? Check (✔) your answers.

...... **1.** Amundsen will get the dogs and begin the journey.

...... **2.** Amundsen will not find the dogs he needs.

...... **3.** Amundsen will tell the men about the change of plan, and they will be angry.

...... **4.** Amundsen will tell the men about the change of plan, and they will be excited.

B. Now read the extract to see what happens.

🎧 *CD 2 Track 13*

Words

The ship's name was *Fram,* and the man was Roald Amundsen. The *Fram* was the most beautiful ship on earth, Amundsen thought. His friends were the best skiers on earth, too. One of them, Olav Bjaaland, smiled at him.

"North Pole, here we come, Captain," he said.

"Yes." Amundsen said. His friends could not see his

50

face in the dark. "*Fram* is going to the Arctic."

Everyone on the *Fram* was ready to go to the North Pole, to the Arctic. Amundsen wanted to go there, too. But first he wanted to go south. His friends didn't know that.

100

At midnight on June 6th, the *Fram* moved quietly away from Amundsen's house, out to sea.

The *Fram* went to an island in the south of Norway. It was a very little island, with only one small wooden house, two trees, and nearly a hundred dogs.

150

"Look at that!" Bjaaland said. "It's an island of dogs! There are dogs in the water, near the trees, on the house—dogs everywhere!"

Two men came out of the house. "Hassel! Lindstrøm!" Amundsen said. "It's good to see you! How many dogs do you have for me?"

200

"Ninety-nine, Roald," said Hassel. "The best ninety-nine dogs from Greenland. And they're very happy! They don't work; they just eat and play all day! They're having a wonderful summer here!"

"Good, good." Amundsen laughed. "But that's finished now. Hey, Bjaaland! Stop laughing—come down here and help me. Let's get all these dogs onto the ship!"

It was not easy. The dogs were fat and strong, and they didn't want to go on the ship. But at last, after three hours' hard work, all ninety-nine were on the ship, and the *Fram* went out to sea again.

The men were not happy. The weather was bad, the dogs were dirty, and some of the men were sick. They began to ask questions.

"Why are we bringing dogs with us?" asked one man, Johansen. "We're going thousands of kilometers south, past Cape Horn, and then north to Alaska. Why not wait, and get dogs in Alaska?"

"Don't ask me," said his friend, Helmer Hanssen, "I don't understand it."

The men talked for a long time. Then, on September 9th, Amundsen called everyone to the back of the ship. He stood quietly and looked at them. Behind him was a big map. It was not a map of the Arctic. It was a map of Antarctica.

Bjaaland looked at Helmer Hanssen, and laughed. Then Amundsen began to speak.

"Boys," he said. "I know you are unhappy. You often ask me difficult questions, and I don't answer. Well, I'm going to answer all those questions now, today.

"We began to work for this journey two years ago. Then, we wanted to be the first men at the North Pole. But last year, Peary, an American, found the North Pole. So America was first to the North Pole, not Norway. We're going there, but we're too late."

"I don't understand this," Bjaaland thought. "Why is Amundsen talking about the North Pole, with a map of Antarctica behind him?"

Amundsen stopped for a minute, and looked at all the men slowly. No one said anything.

"We have to go a long way south before we get to

250

300

350

400

450

500

Alaska," he said. "Very near Antarctica, you know. And Captain Scott, the Englishman, is going to the South Pole this year. He wants to put his British flag there. An American flag at the North Pole, a British flag at the South Pole."

Bjaaland began to understand. He started to smile and couldn't stop. He was warm and excited.

"Well, boys," Amundsen said slowly. "Do we want the British to put their flag at the South Pole first? How fast can we travel? We have a lot of dogs, and some of the most wonderful skiers on earth—Bjaaland here is the best in Norway! So I have an idea, boys. Let's go to the South Pole, and put the Norwegian flag there before the British! What do you say?"

For a minute or two it was very quiet. Amundsen waited, and the men watched him and thought. Then Bjaaland laughed.

"Yes!" he said. "Why not? It's a ski race, isn't it, and the English can't ski! It's a wonderful idea, of course! Let's go!"

Extract from *The Coldest Place on Earth,* Bookworms Library, Oxford University Press.

After Reading

Answer the questions.

1. Where do Amundsen's friends think they're going?

   ....

2. Which country's flag is already at the North Pole?

   ....

3. What is Olav Bjaaland good at doing?

   ....

4. Who is Captain Scott?

   ....

Thinking About the Story

A. **Answer the questions.**

1. Did you enjoy reading the extract? Do you want to read more about the race to the South Pole?
2. Do you think Amundsen and his men will get to the South Pole before the British?
3. Do you think all of the men and dogs will reach the South Pole?

B. **Discuss your answer with your classmates.**

Timed Repeated Reading

How many words can you read in one minute? Follow the instructions to practice increasing your reading speed.

1. Time yourself. Read the extract for one minute. When you stop, underline the last word you read and write "first" in the margin.
2. Go back to the beginning of the extract. Read again for one minute. Try to read faster this time. When you stop, underline the last word you read and write "second" in the margin.
3. Go back to the beginning of the extract. Read again for one minute. Try to read even faster this time. When you stop, underline the last word you read and write "third" in the margin.
4. Count the number of words you read each time. Record the three numbers on the Timed Repeated Reading Chart on page 169.

Unit 11

Challenges

Discuss the questions.

1. What is the most challenging job you can think of?
2. What challenges have you faced in your life?

This unit is about people who have faced challenges—they have managed to do difficult things. In Part 1, you will read about a university student's experience in a summer job. In Part 2, you will read about a successful athlete. The unit is followed by Extensive Reading 11, which is an extract from a book called *The Little Princess*. It is about a little girl who has to face the challenge of a new life in a foreign country.

Before Reading

Discuss the questions.

1. Have you ever had a summer job?
2. What did you learn from it?

Comprehension Strategy: Recognizing Points of View

A point of view is an opinion. In some texts, the writer expresses his or her own opinion. In others, the writer summarizes other people's points of view instead. Look for words like *according to*, *says*, *believes*, and *thinks*.

A. Read the text. Match the people with the points of view.

..... **1.** Rob Walker   **a.** Rob helped the residents.

..... **2.** Rob's parents   **b.** The residents helped Rob learn a lesson.

B. Read the whole text and answer the questions that follow.

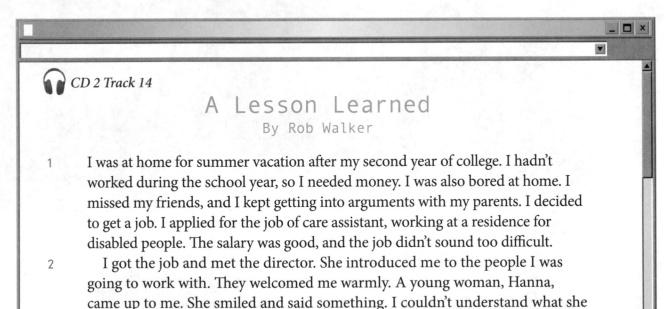

CD 2 Track 14

A Lesson Learned
By Rob Walker

1   I was at home for summer vacation after my second year of college. I hadn't worked during the school year, so I needed money. I was also bored at home. I missed my friends, and I kept getting into arguments with my parents. I decided to get a job. I applied for the job of care assistant, working at a residence for disabled people. The salary was good, and the job didn't sound too difficult.

2   I got the job and met the director. She introduced me to the people I was going to work with. They welcomed me warmly. A young woman, Hanna, came up to me. She smiled and said something. I couldn't understand what she said. "What?" I asked. She repeated herself. I still didn't understand. I realized she had a speech disability. I felt embarrassed, so I pretended that I knew what she was saying. I just said, "Yes" to her. She seemed to think my answer was very funny.

3   Ken was another resident. He was my age, but he looked a lot older. He was in a wheelchair, but he seemed to have no problems getting around. He showed me around the place and told me what I needed to do. At first, I felt a bit uncomfortable. I wasn't used to dealing with people with disabilities. The job seemed more challenging than I first thought.

4   After I had worked there for a while, I got to know some of the residents really well. I also found out why Hanna had laughed at me when I started. The question she had asked me was, "What is your name?" I had replied, "Yes" because I hadn't understood the question. She called me "Mr. Yes" after that as a joke.

5   Helping at meals was my most difficult task. I needed to be very patient. Most of the residents had trouble eating. But whatever their physical challenges were, they rarely complained.

6   I couldn't help comparing their behavior with mine. I thought of all the times I argued with my parents and complained about things like tidying my room. Now I realize I don't really have much to complain about. I should be grateful for what I have.

7   I worked at the residence for three months. My parents were pleased. They felt I was helping people who needed help. But actually, the residents were the ones who helped me. They helped me learn one of the most valuable lessons of my life.

Checking Comprehension

A. Complete the sentences.

1. The author wrote this because ....
   a. he wanted to explain how to become a care assistant.
   b. he wanted to explain how he learned a lesson.
   c. he wanted to show he was good at his job.

2. Rob took the job of care assistant mainly ....
   a. because he wanted a challenge.
   b. because he wanted to help people.
   c. because he needed money.

3. When Hanna asked Rob what his name was, ...
   a. he replied, "Yes" because he was joking.
   b. he replied, "Yes" because he couldn't understand what she said.
   c. he replied, "Rob."

4. Hanna called Rob "Mr. Yes" because ....
   a. she thought "Mr. Yes" was his name.
   b. she couldn't pronounce his name.
   c. she was joking with him.

5. Rob's parents were pleased because ....
   a. they thought he learned a valuable lesson.
   b. they felt he was helping people.
   c. he stopped complaining about everything.

6. The valuable lesson Rob learned was that ....
   a. he should be grateful for what he had.
   b. the residents didn't often complain about things.
   c. the job was more difficult than he first thought.

Looking at Vocabulary in Context

A. **Find the words in bold in the text. Circle the correct definitions.**

1. A **residence** (par. 1) means *a place where people live / a workplace.*

2. Someone who is **disabled** (par. 1) is *not able to use part of their body properly / not able to work.*

3. If you feel **embarrassed,** (par. 2) you feel *confident and happy / worried and uncomfortable.*

4. If you **pretended** (par. 2) to do something, you *told the truth / lied.*

5. If you **complained** (par. 5) about something, you said you were *happy about it / unhappy about it.*

6. Something that is **valuable** (par. 7) is *important and worth a lot / unimportant and not worth much.*

B. **Fill in the blanks with the words in bold from A. Use the correct forms.**

1. I was really _____ when I sneezed loudly in a quiet room.

2. The White House is the official _____ of the American president.

3. You should keep _____ jewelry in a safe place.

4. If your soup is cold, you should _____ to the waiter.

5. My friends all _____ to forget my birthday, but they were really planning a surprise party for me.

6. The new train doors are designed so that _____ people can get on and get off more easily.

What's Your Opinion?

A. **Answer the questions for yourself.**

	You	Your Partner
1. Do you think Rob seems like a nice person at the beginning of the story?	....	....
2. Do you think Rob seems like a nice person at the end of the story?	....	....
3. Do you think Rob helped the people at the residence?	....	....
4. Do you think Rob will work at the residence again next summer?	....	....
5. Do you think Rob will do a different job next summer?	....	....

B. **Ask a partner the same questions. Discuss your answers. Give reasons for your answers.**

Before Reading

Discuss the questions.

1. Who is the most famous athlete in your country?
2. Do you know what the Paralympics are?

Fluency Strategy: Ignoring Unknown Words

To understand what the writer is saying, you don't need to know the meaning of every word. Put your dictionary away. When you come to words you don't know, ignore them. Keep reading. Think about what you can understand, not what you can't.

A. **Use the strategy to read the text. Complete the information.**

1. Name: _Chantal Petitclerc_
2. Occupation: _____
3. Nationality: _____
4. Number of world records: _____

B. **Read the whole text quickly. Record your reading time below and in the chart on page 169.**

CD 2 Track 15

Start: _____
Finish: _____
Reading Time: _____

An Amazing Athlete

1   One of the best female athletes in the world is Canadian Chantal Petitclerc. She holds world records and has won many gold medals. Chantal has had amazing success even though she cannot walk.

2   Chantal is a wheelchair racing specialist. When she was 13 years old, she lost the use of both legs in an accident. Chantal was not very athletic as a child. However, after her accident she decided to find a physical activity to stay in shape, so she took up swimming. She started wheelchair racing in 1987. In her first wheelchair race, at the age of 18, she finished last. This did not stop her. Instead, Chantal fell in love with the sport and started training.

3   Five years later, Chantal took part in the Paralympic Games. In the Paralympics, the best disabled athletes around the world compete against each

other. Like the Olympics, the Games take place every four years. At her first Paralympics, in Spain, Chantal won two bronze medals. She has also taken part in the 1996, 2000, and 2004 Paralympic Games. So far, Chantal has won 11 Paralympic medals and set three world records.

4

Chantal Petitclerc

Chantal's achievements have made her famous in Canada. In 2004, a Canadian magazine named her "Canadian of the Year." Despite her fame and success, Chantal seems to have a very normal life. She is serious about training, but she doesn't let it take over her life. She never trains after six o'clock at night. Her favorite activities include reading and watching movies. She also likes having quiet dinners with friends. She lives in an apartment in Montreal, Canada, with her boyfriend. She says they are both very independent. They share household chores, like cooking, fifty-fifty. She says she learned most household jobs in a wheelchair. She can't even imagine what it's like to take out the trash or to go shopping standing up.

5   Chantal was at the University of Alberta when she first decided to start training for the Paralympics. She was studying for a history degree. She wanted to finish her studies, but she had to make a choice between staying at the university and training for the Paralympics. Chantal is happy with her choice, but she would like to finish her degree some day. Given what she has done with her life so far, it should be easy for her to take on another challenge.

Checking Fluency and Comprehension

A. **Complete the sentences. Do not look back at the text.**

1. Chantal Petitclerc has been interested in sports ....
   a. since she was a small child.
   b. since she had an accident.

2. Chantal started wheelchair racing ....
   a. to stay in shape.
   b. to make money.

3. In her first wheelchair race, ...
   a. she won a medal.
   b. she came in last.

4. Chantal has won ....
   a. 11 Paralympic medals.
   b. two Olympic medals.

5. Chantal didn't finish her degree because she was ....
   a. training for the Paralympics.
   b. bored with studying.

B. **Check your answers with a partner. Record your score on page 169.**

Expanding Vocabulary

A. **Verbs with two or more parts are called phrasal verbs. Find the phrasal verbs in bold in the text. Then match the halves of the definitions.**

.... 1. If you **took** something **up** (par. 2),
.... 2. If events **take place** (par. 3),
.... 3. If you **took part in** an activity (par. 3),
.... 4. If something starts to **take over** (par. 4),
.... 5. If you **take** something **out** (par. 4),
.... 6. If you **take** something **on** (par. 5),

a. you participated in it with other people.
b. you remove it.
c. you started a new sport or hobby.
d. it is in control.
e. they happen.
f. you decide to do something difficult.

B. Fill in the blanks with the phrasal verbs from A. Use the correct forms.

1. The concert will _____ in the park on Saturday.

2. I'd like to _____ snowboarding, as I'm already a good skier.

3. The head of the company just left, and no one knows who will _____ as the new director.

4. My brother cleaned the kitchen, and I _____ the bathroom.

5. We're having the chicken tonight, so I must _____ it _____ of the freezer.

6. I hurt my leg playing basketball last week, so I can't _____ the game today.

What's Your Opinion?

A. Do you agree or disagree with the statements? Check (✔) your answers.

	Agree	Disagree	Not Sure
1. I enjoy doing things that are challenging and difficult.	☐	☐	☐
2. I prefer to do things that I already know how to do.	☐	☐	☐
3. I enjoy doing things that are new and different.	☐	☐	☐
4. If I don't succeed in something the first time, I usually don't try again.	☐	☐	☐
5. If I don't succeed in something the first time, I keep trying until I improve.	☐	☐	☐

B. Discuss your answers with a partner. Give reasons for your answers.

Increasing Fluency

Scan the line to find the word on the left. Words may appear more than once. Can you finish in 15 seconds?

	a	b	c	d	e
1. sport	sprout	sports	sport	spot	sport
2. racing	racing	lacing	raking	raring	racing
3. quiet	quite	greet	quiet	quiet	quell
4. split	split	spill	spilt	split	sprint
5. choice	choose	choice	chose	voice	choice
6. trash	trash	thrash	brash	trash	flash
7. shape	scrape	share	shape	shade	shale
8. trains	plains	train	slain	trains	trains

Extensive Reading 11

A Little Princess

Introduction

This extract from an Oxford *Bookworms* reader gives you the opportunity to read more in English. The more you read, the faster and more fluent you will become. *A Little Princess* is set in England in the 19th century. The story is about a little girl named Sara Crewe. She was born in India. Her father decides she should go to Miss Minchin's school in England. Sara is sad when her father goes back to India to work. One girl at the school, Lavinia, is not very nice to her, but Sara has some good friends like Ermengarde. The extract you will read starts with Sara getting a letter from her father.

Before Reading

A. What do you think will happen in the extract? Check (✔) your answers.

...... **1.** Mr. Crewe's letter asks Sara to return to India.

...... **2.** Mr. Crewe's letter tells Sara that she will be very rich.

...... **3.** Mr. Crewe's letter tells Sara that he has lost all his money.

...... **4.** Mr. Crewe's letter tells Sara he is coming to live in England.

B. Now read the extract to see what happens.

🎧 *CD 2 Track 16*

Words

One day a very exciting letter arrived. Everybody in the school talked about it for days.

"*My friend,*" wrote Mr. Crewe, "*has some mines in northern India, and a month ago his workers found diamonds there. There are thousands of diamonds in these mines, but it is expensive work to get them out. My friend*   50 *needs my help. So, Little Missus'* (this was Mr. Crewe's special name for Sara), "*I am putting all my money into my friend's diamond mines, and one day you and I are going to be very rich…*"

Sara was not interested in money, but a story about   100 diamond mines in India was exciting. Nearly everybody was very pleased for Sara, but not Lavinia, of course.

"Huh!" she said. "My mother has a diamond. Lots of people have diamonds. What's so interesting about diamond mines?"

"But there are thousands of diamonds in these mines," said Ermengarde. "Perhaps millions of them!"

Lavinia laughed. "Is Sara going to wear diamonds in her hair at breakfast, then? Or is it 'Princess Sara' now?"

Sara's face went red. She looked at Lavinia angrily, but said quietly, "Some people call me 'princess.' I know that. But princesses don't get angry or say unkind things, so I'm not going to say anything to you, Lavinia."

"To me, you *are* a princess," Ermengarde said to Sara later. "And you always look like a princess, in your beautiful dresses."

Sara was a princess to another girl, too. This was Becky. She was a servant in Miss Minchin's school, and she was only fourteen years old, but she worked all day and sometimes half the night. She carried things upstairs and downstairs, she cleaned the floors, she made the fires, and she was always tired and hungry and dirty. She and Sara had very different lives.

But one day Sara came into her bedroom, and there was Becky, sleeping in a chair.

"Oh, you poor thing!" Sara said.

Then Becky opened her eyes and saw Sara. She got up at once. "Oh, Miss!" she said. "I'm very sorry, Miss! I just sat down for a minute and—"

"Don't be afraid," said Sara. She gave Becky a friendly smile. "You were tired. That's all."

"Are you—are you going to tell Miss Minchin?" asked Becky. She began to move to the door.

"Of course not," said Sara. "Please don't run away. Sit down again for a minute. You look so tired."

"Oh, Miss, I can't!" Becky said. "You're very kind, Miss, but Miss Minchin—"

"Please," said Sara. She took Becky's hand. "You're only a little girl, like me. Let's be friends."

And so Becky sat down again, and soon she and Sara were friends. Nobody knew about this, of course. Rich little girls at Miss Minchin's school did not make friends with servant-girls, and it was a wonderful thing for Becky. Nearly every day she and Sara met in Sara's bedroom, just for five or ten minutes. Becky was always hungry, and Sara often bought nice things for her to eat. They sat and talked, and sometimes Sara told Becky some of her stories. Becky loved that.

"Oh, Miss," she said. "You tell them so beautifully! Sometimes I like your stories better than things to eat."

And after those visits to Sara's room, Becky always felt better—not so tired, and not so hungry.

Some months later Sara had her eleventh birthday. Lessons stopped for the afternoon and there was a big party for all the girls in the school.

"This party is expensive for us," Miss Minchin said to her sister Amelia. "But it looks good for the school."

That afternoon there was a visitor to the school—Miss Minchin's lawyer. He went with Miss Minchin into her office and they closed the door. In the schoolroom next door there was a lot of noise from Sara's party. Everybody in there was very happy.

But in the office Miss Minchin was not happy. She looked at the lawyer angrily. "What are you saying? Mr. Crewe has no money? What about the diamond mines?"

"There are *no* diamond mines," said the lawyer. "Well, there are mines, but there are no diamonds in them."

"But Mr. Crewe's good friend—" began Miss Minchin.

"Mr. Crewe's good friend," said the lawyer, "ran away

450

500

550

600

650

700

with all Mr. Crewe's money. Ralph Crewe was ill with a fever, and when he heard about this, he got worse. A week later he was dead."

"Dead!" cried Miss Minchin. "But what about his daughter Sara? And this expensive birthday party?'

"Sara Crewe has no money," said the lawyer. "Not a penny in the world, Miss Minchin. Not a penny."

"She must leave my school at once," Miss Minchin said angrily. "She must go this afternoon!"

Extract from *A Little Princess,* Bookworms Library, Oxford University Press.

750

Total Words: 795

After Reading

Answer the questions.

1. According to Mr. Crewe's letter, what will make them very rich?

   ....

2. Who is Becky?

   ....

3. Why did the school have a party?

   ....

4. What happened to Mr. Crewe?

   ....

Thinking About the Story

Answer the questions.

1. Did you enjoy reading the extract? Do you want to read more about Sara?
2. Do you like Miss Minchin? Why or why not?
3. What do you think will happen to Sara?

Timed Repeated Reading

How many words can you read in one minute? Follow the instructions to practice increasing your reading speed.

1. Time yourself. Read the extract for one minute. When you stop, underline the last word you read and write "first" in the margin.
2. Go back to the beginning of the extract. Read again for one minute. Try to read faster this time. When you stop, underline the last word you read and write "second" in the margin.
3. Go back to the beginning of the extract. Read again for one minute. Try to read even faster this time. When you stop, underline the last word you read and write "third" in the margin.
4. Count the number of words you read each time. Record the three numbers on the Timed Repeated Reading Chart on page 169.

Space

Discuss the questions.

1. Do you think there is life on other planets?
2. Would you like to travel in space?

This unit is about space and space travel. In Part 1, you will read about UFOs (Unidentified Flying Objects). In Part 2, you will read about becoming a space tourist. The unit is followed by Extensive Reading 12, which is an extract from a book called *Under the Moon*. It is set in the year 2522, where people travel in spaceships and the Earth is in danger.

Part 1 UFOs: Are They Out There?

Before Reading

Discuss the questions.

1. What does the photo on page 157 show?
2. Does the photo prove that UFOs are real?

Comprehension Strategy: Finding Main Ideas in Paragraphs

Every paragraph has a main idea. This is the most important thing the writer wants to say. The main idea is often near the beginning of the paragraph.

A. **Read the text. Write the paragraph number with its main idea.**

  5 **a.** Many people in different places have described similar objects.

  _____ **b.** Skeptics don't believe UFOs are visitors from other planets.

  _____ **c.** A UFO incident took place at a military base in China.

  _____ **d.** Many people believe UFOs are visitors from other planets.

  _____ **e.** The number of UFO reports increased at the end of the 20th century.

B. **Read the text again and answer the questions that follow.**

🎧 *CD 2 Track 17*

UFOs: Are They Out There?

1   As the twentieth century came to an end, something strange seemed to be happening in the skies. Reports of UFOs, or "Unidentified Flying Objects," suddenly increased. Many of these reports came from China.

2   One of the most dramatic UFO reports came in October 1998. It took place at a military base in the northern province of Hebei. Four radar stations reported an unidentified object in the sky. Over 140 people on the ground said they saw the UFO. They said it looked like a small star. A Chinese air force plane was ordered to intercept the UFO. When the plane got close to the UFO, the object moved quickly away. The two pilots of the plane kept trying to get closer to the UFO. Each time they were about 4,000 meters from it, the UFO quickly flew away. The plane had to return to its base because it was running out of fuel.

3   Many people believe UFOs are visitors from other planets. One survey found that 50 percent of the Chinese population believes UFOs come from outer space. The percentage is similar in the United States. They point to thousands of sightings as evidence. In some cases, many witnesses say they have seen the same thing at the same time. Many airline pilots have reported seeing UFOs. Around one in seven Americans say they, or someone they know, have seen a UFO. How could all these people be wrong? Finally, they say hundreds of photos of strange objects in the sky prove UFOs exist.

4   Skeptics believe there are rational explanations for UFOs. They say many witnesses just don't understand what they see. The objects that they see are not visitors from outer space. They are really ordinary things like airplane lights, or unusual weather conditions. In addition, skeptics say many reports of UFOs are hoaxes. It is easy to create fake photographs, especially with digital images.

5   Many people in different places have described seeing similar objects. Most of the early reports, in the 1940s, described things that looked like "flying saucers." They were flat and round, with bright lights. In the 1980s, many people also started describing UFOs shaped like triangles. Believers say this shows people are all seeing the same things. Skeptics say people are just describing UFOs from movies. For example, the Chinese air force pilots said the object they saw looked like UFOs from foreign movies. To find out what UFOs will look like in the twenty-first century, maybe we should visit a movie theater.

Checking Comprehension

A. Mark the statements true (T) or false (F). Correct the ones which are false.

.... 1. The topic of the article is UFOs.

....

.... 2. The Chinese plane finally returned to the base because the UFO disappeared.

....

.... 3. About half the people in China believe UFOs come from outer space.

....

.... 4. About half the people in the United States say they, or someone they know, have
         seen a UFO.

....

.... 5. People who don't believe in UFOs say the witnesses are all lying.

....

.... 6. UFOs are sometimes called flying saucers because they are flat and round.

....

B. What do the two groups of people say about each piece of evidence? Complete the
chart with the missing information.

	People who believe in UFOs say ...	People who don't believe in UFOs say ...
1. Number of witness reports	How could all these people be wrong?	
2. Photographs		
3. Similar UFO descriptions		

Looking at Vocabulary in Context

A. Find the words in bold in the text. Circle the word or phrase with the closest meaning.

1. **dramatic** (par. 2)

   a. ordinary   **b.** amazing

2. **intercept** (par. 2)

   a. stop   **b.** shoot down

3. **evidence** (par. 3)

   a. facts   **b.** money

4. **witnesses** (par. 3)

   a. onlookers   **b.** skeptics

5. **rational** (par. 4)

   a. crazy   **b.** reasonable

6. **hoaxes** (par. 4)

   a. tricks   **b.** facts

B. Fill in the blanks with the words in bold from A. Use the correct forms.

1. A _____ to the robbery said she saw two men in a car outside the bank.

2. A lot of scientific _____ links smoking to heart disease.

3. Governments can use spying technology to _____ emails and phone calls.

4. I got an email saying I had won a thousand dollars, but sadly it was just a _____.

5. The police made a _____ rescue using a helicopter.

6. I am very angry about losing my job, but I must calm down and make a _____ decision about my future.

What's Your Opinion?

A. Interview other people in your class. For each question, find someone who answers "Yes" and write their name.

Name

1. Do you believe UFOs are travelers from other planets?   _____

2. Do you think UFO reports are often hoaxes?   _____

3. Would you like to see a UFO?   _____

4. Do you know someone who has seen a UFO?   _____

5. Would you like to find out more about UFOs?   _____

B. Tell the rest of the class what you found out.

Part 2

A Ticket to Outer Space

Before Reading

Discuss the questions.

1. How much do you think a ticket to the far side of the moon would cost?
2. When do you think ordinary people will be able to buy trips to space?

Fluency Strategy: Recognizing Signal Words

Signal words show how the text is organized. *First of all* introduces the first in a series of points. *Secondly* and *thirdly* give more information about the subject. *Finally* gives the last point.

A. Paragraph 4 lists some problems with space travel. Scan for the signal words and match them with the problems.

...... **1.** First of all	**a.** physical effects on the body
...... **2.** Secondly	**b.** amount of training and preparation
...... **3.** Thirdly	**c.** practical difficulties caused by lack of gravity
...... **4.** Finally	**d.** cost of space travel

B. Read the whole text quickly. Record your reading time below and in the chart on page 169.

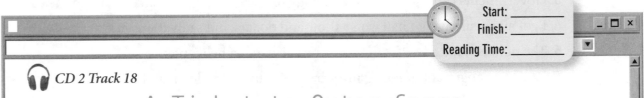

Start: _____
Finish: _____
Reading Time: _____

🎧 *CD 2 Track 18*

A Ticket to Outer Space

1   A dramatic moment in world history took place on July 20, 1969, with one small step. That was when Neil Armstrong became the first person to walk on the moon. Since then, many people have dreamed of traveling into space.

2   Some companies are now offering to make this dream come true—for a price. They are selling tickets for trips into space on the Russian spacecraft Soyuz. A few people have already taken these trips, or "space tours" as they have been called. The space tourists stay at the International Space Station, a large space research center which rotates around the earth. The program lasts just over a week, and tourists are able to go around the Earth 120 times and travel millions of kilometers.

3   More space tours are planned for the near future. One tour plans to take space travelers around the far side of the moon and back to Earth. The space travelers will be able to view Earth and the moon from the windows of the craft. Many people say that they would like to take these tours.

4   However, before everyone starts lining up to get a ticket, there are some things to consider. First of all, there is the price. The cost for the trip to the far side of the moon will be about 100 million dollars. Secondly, there is the amount of training and preparation required for space flights. The tours require all travelers to train for six months before they can take the trip. They must also get in shape so that they pass the medical examinations. Thirdly, the lack of gravity in space means that practical activities become difficult. Everything is weightless. Everyone and anything that is not tied down will float. It is not possible to sit, walk, or lie down. It is impossible to do simple things like taking a shower. You cannot use water or shampoo because liquids float. Instead, people use a wet, soapy cloth to wash. Finally, there are the physical effects on the body. The lack of gravity causes blood to flow toward the head. As a result, people get terrible headaches. Also, their bones and muscles become weak because there is no gravity to push against them. To stay fit, space travelers need to exercise several hours each day.

5   Space exploration is not yet for everyone. It is a true adventure, but like all adventures, it has its challenges.

Checking Fluency and Comprehension

A. **Answer the questions. Do not look back at the passage.**

1. Why do you think this article was written?
   a. To try to get people to buy trips into space.
   b. To tell people about the challenges of being a space tourist.

2. What is described as one of the greatest moments in world history?
   a. When Neil Armstrong walked on the moon.
   b. When companies began to sell space tours.

3. What can people do on a space tour?
   a. Operate a spacecraft and take an examination.
   b. Travel around the Earth and stay at a space station.

4. Why is it impossible to lie in bed in space?
   a. Because everything in space is weightless.
   b. Because people get terrible headaches.

5. Why will space travelers need to exercise every day?
   a. Because they will take space walks.
   b. Because their bones and muscles will become weak.

B. **Check your answers with a partner. Record your score on page 169.**

Expanding Vocabulary

A. **Find the missing verbs and nouns in the text. Complete the chart.**

Noun	Verb
1. rotation	...........................(par. 2)
2. consideration	...........................(par. 4)
3. flotation	...........................(par. 4)
4. ....(par. 4)	prepare
5. ....(par. 4)	examine
6. ....(par. 5)	explore

B. Fill in the blanks with the verbs or nouns from A. Use the correct forms.

1. An empty bottle will .... on water.

2. Sonja stayed late at the library because she had to study for her history ....

3. There are many points you should .... before you decide to buy a house.

4. How many .... does the Earth make around the Sun each year?

5. It takes a lot of time and effort to .... for a trip into space.

6. The first .... of Mars occurred in the 1960s.

What's Your Opinion?

A. Do you agree or disagree with the statements? Check (✔) your answers.

	Agree	Disagree	Not Sure
1. I would like to go to space if tickets become cheaper in the future.	☐	☐	☐
2. I wouldn't like to go to space because of the physical effects.	☐	☐	☐
3. I would enjoy floating in space without gravity.	☐	☐	☐
4. I wouldn't like to do six months of space training.	☐	☐	☐
5. I would enjoy training to go to space.	☐	☐	☐

B. Discuss your answers with a partner. Give reasons for your answers.

Increasing Fluency

Scan the line to find the word on the left. Words may appear more than once. Can you finish in 15 seconds?

	a	b	c	d	e
1. true	true	blue	rue	true	lure
2. space	spaces	paces	space	capes	space
3. soapy	soupy	soapy	ropy	copy	dopey
4. tied	tied	lied	tried	teed	tied
5. center	renter	central	center	sender	fender
6. blood	brood	blood	booed	blood	hood
7. moon	moon	noon	room	moor	moon
8. tours	sour	tools	store	tours	tour

Extensive Reading 12

Under the Moon

Introduction

This extract from an Oxford *Bookworms* reader gives you the opportunity to read more in English. The more you read, the faster and more fluent you will become. *Under the Moon* is set in the future, in the year 2522. It is about two people, Kiah and Rilla, who work on a space ship, OM-45. They learn that the Earth is in danger, because the Artificial Ozone Layer, the AOL, is breaking up. If the AOL breaks up, the Earth will burn up from the heat of the sun. But the leaders on Earth don't want to hear about the problem. The last person who tried to warn them, a man called Adai, was sent to a moon colony as a punishment. How will Kiah and Rilla make the leader of Earth, Gog, listen to them? They think the leader of Australia, Commander Zadak, might help. The extract you will read begins as they travel to Earth to meet with Commander Zadak.

Before Reading

A. What do you think will happen in the extract? Check (✔) your answers.

...... 1. Kiah and Rilla meet Zadak and he agrees to help them.

...... 2. Kiah and Rilla meet Zadak, but he does not believe that Earth will die.

...... 3. Kiah and Rilla travel to Earth and find it is already getting hotter from the sun.

...... 4. Kiah and Rilla cannot meet Zadak because Earth is destroyed.

B. **Now read the extract to see what happens.**

Words

 CD 2 Track 19

On Friday, after three weeks in space, Kiah and Rilla finished work and left Ship OM-45 on a space plane to Kisangani. Kiah called Adai and Rilla called Commander Zadak in Australia. The next morning they took an airplane to Sydney. A taxi took them from the airport to Commander Zadak's office, some kilometers north of Sydney.

50

"Wait for us here," Kiah said to the taxi driver.

Kiah and Rilla walked to the gate. About ten guards stood in front of the gate. Across the road, a train waited.

"Rilla, OM–45," Rilla said. "To see Commander Zadak at four-thirty."

"Let me call the Commander's office," the guard said.

Kiah and Rilla waited. It was hot, and Kiah began to feel thirsty.

The guard came back. "I'm sorry," he said. "The Commander can't see you."

"But I talked to the Commander yesterday," Rilla said. "He wanted to see us at four-thirty."

"The Commander is leaving on the train in three minutes," the guard said.

"Can we wait and see him here?" Kiah asked.

"No!" the guard shouted. "Get out of here!"

Kiah and Rilla walked back to the taxi.

"Where's the driver?" Kiah asked.

"Look! He's sitting by that wall," Rilla said.

Just then, Commander Zadak came out of the gate. He was a very tall, big man with blue eyes and a lot of white hair. Two guards marched in front of him, and two guards marched behind him. They all carried guns.

"There he is!" Rilla cried. "Commander!" And she began to run along the road to him. 250

Commander Zadak did not stop. A guard opened the door of the train and the Commander got in. Slowly, the train began to move.

Kiah ran to the taxi and jumped in. Then he drove the taxi fast down the road. The taxi driver saw him and ran 300 after him. The train began to move faster. Suddenly, Kiah drove the taxi off the road. He drove in front of the train and stopped.

The train came nearer. And then the train stopped, very near the taxi, and some guards jumped off. Kiah opened 350 the door and got out of the taxi.

"Put up your hands!" the guards shouted.

Two of the guards began to hit Kiah.

"Stop that!" someone shouted. "Bring him over here!" It was Commander Zadak.

Kiah stood in front of the Commander. Just then, Rilla arrived.

"Oh, it's you!" Commander Zadak said. He did not 400 smile. "Rilla, your father's going to be angry."

"We want to talk to you, Commander," Rilla said. "It's very important."

"Very well. I'm listening."

Kiah began to talk. "Two years ago, Adai told you about the holes in the AOL. Now they're worse. The AOL 450 is breaking up over Europe. Please look at these numbers and this satellite picture."

He gave his book to Commander Zadak, and the Commander looked at the numbers.

"It's important, Commander," Kiah said. "In ten years Earth is going to die."

"You stopped my train because of this?" Commander Zadak asked. "Two years ago Adai talked to me about the AOL. Then he talked to Earth Commander, and what happened? Where is Adai now? Is the Moon colony helping the AOL?"

"We know about Adai, Commander," Rilla said. "But someone needs to talk to Earth Commander again."

"I'm going to talk to Gog about rain, I can tell you that. Earth needs rain; there was no rain last winter. Half of Australia has no water, and my trees here are dying. Without rain, many people are going to die. Is Gog going to understand that? I don't know!"

Commander Zadak began to walk back to his train. "Move that taxi!" he called to his guards.

Some guards moved the taxi back to the road and then they jumped on to the train again. The train began to move.

"OK," the taxi driver shouted. "What are you going to do next? Drive my taxi into the river?"

Kiah smiled. He took some money from his pocket and gave it to the taxi driver.

The taxi driver looked at the money. "OK, OK," he said. "Where now? Back to the airport?"

Kiah took Rilla's hand. "Yes," he said. "Let's get back to Kisangani. We can call Adai again tomorrow."

Extract from *Under the Moon,* Bookworms Library, Oxford University Press.

After Reading

Answer the questions.

1. Why do the guards say Kiah and Rilla can't meet with Zadak?

....

2. How did Kiah make the train stop?

....

3. According to Kiah, when will Earth die?

....

4. According to Zadak, what does Earth need?

....

Thinking About the Story

Answer the questions.

1. Did you enjoy reading the extract? Do you want to read more about 2522 and the danger to the Earth?
2. Do you think Kiah and Rilla will stop the Earth from being destroyed?
3. Do you think Earth will really be like this in the year 2522?

Timed Repeated Reading

How many words can you read in one minute? Follow the instructions to practice increasing your reading speed.

1. Time yourself. Read the extract for one minute. When you stop, underline the last word you read and write "first" in the margin.
2. Go back to the beginning of the extract. Read again for one minute. Try to read faster this time. When you stop, underline the last word you read and write "second" in the margin.
3. Go back to the beginning of the extract. Read again for one minute. Try to read even faster this time. When you stop, underline the last word you read and write "third" in the margin.
4. Count the number of words you read each time. Record the three numbers on the Timed Repeated Reading Chart on page 169.

Reading Rate Chart

Time \ Unit	1	2	3	4	5	6	7	8	9	10	11	12	Rate (words per minute)
1:00													400
1:15													320
1:30													267
1:45													229
2:00													200
2:15													178
2:30													160
2:45													145
3:00													133
3:15													123
3:30													114
3:45													107
4:00													100
4:15													94
4:30													89
4:45													84
5:00													80
5:15													76
5:30													73
5:45													70
6:00													67
6:15													64
6:30													62
6:45													59
7:00													57
7:15													55
7:30													53
7:45													51
8:00													50
Question score (out of 5)													

Timed Repeated Reading Chart

Extensive Reading	1	2	3	4	5	6	7	8	9	10	11	12
1st try												
2nd try												
3rd try												

Vocabulary Index

OXFORD
UNIVERSITY PRESS

198 Madison Avenue
New York, NY 10016 USA

Great Clarendon Street, Oxford OX2 6DP UK

Oxford University Press is a department of the University of Oxford.
It furthers the University's objective of excellence in research, scholarship,
and education by publishing worldwide in

Oxford   New York

Auckland   Cape Town   Dar es Salaam   Hong Kong   Karachi
Kuala Lumpur   Madrid   Melbourne   Mexico City   Nairobi
New Delhi   Shanghai   Taipei   Toronto

With offices in

Argentina   Austria   Brazil   Chile   Czech Republic   France   Greece
Guatemala   Hungary   Italy   Japan   Poland   Portugal   Singapore
South Korea   Switzerland   Thailand   Turkey   Ukraine   Vietnam

OXFORD and OXFORD ENGLISH are registered trademarks of
Oxford University Press

© Oxford University Press 2007

Database right Oxford University Press (maker)

No unauthorized photocopying

Market Development Director: Chris Balderston
Senior Editor: Anna Teevan
Assistant Editor: Kate Schubert
Art Director: Maj-Britt Hagsted
Senior Designer: Mia Gomez
Art Editor: Robin Fadool
Production Manager: Shanta Persaud
Production Controller: Eve Wong

STUDENT BOOK ISBN-13: 978 0 19 475813 0

Printed in Hong Kong

Printing (last digit) 10   9   8   7   6   5   4   3   2   1

Acknowledgments:

We would like to thank the following for permission to reproduce photographs:
Cover photograph: Veer
Interior photographs: Masterfile: 1; Agefoto Stock/Digital Vision: 2;
Agefoto Stock/Pixland: Michel Touraine, 7; Agefoto Stock: Marko Turk,
15; Masterfile: Horst Herget, 17; Photo Edit Inc.: Mary Kate Denny, 21;
Photo Researchers: Will & Deni McIntyre, 29; The Image Works: Charles
Walker/Topfoto, 31; Getty Images: Jana Leon, 35; Photo Edit Inc.: Bill
Aron 35; Index Stock: 43; Peter Arnold: 45; Photo Edit Inc.: David Young-
Wolff, 49; Getty Images: Erin Patrice O'Brien, 49; Photo Edit Inc.: David
Young-Wolff, 57; Photo Edit Inc.: David Young-Wolff, 59; Getty Images:
Charles Gupton, 63; Masterfile: Dan Lim, 71; AFP/Getty Images: George
Gobet, 73; Poppy Berry, 77; AFP/Getty Images: Michael Urban, 85; AFP/
Getty Images: 87; AFP/Getty Images: 91; Masterfile: 99; Masterfile: Chad
Johnston, 101; Getty Images: Butch Martin, 105; Masterfile: 113; Punch
Stock/Asiapix, 115; Masterfile: Marc Vaughn, 119; Photo Researchers:
Daniel Zirinsky, 127; Getty Images: Alexander Joe, 129; Reuters: 133; Getty
Images/National Geographic Society: Eduardo Rubiano-Moncad, 137; The
Granger Collection: 139; Agefoto Stock/Creatas: 141; Photo Edit Inc.: Tony
Freeman, 143; Getty Images: Ryan Pierse, 147; Agefoto Stock/Stocktrek:
155; Masterfile: Dave Robertson, 157; PhotoTake/NASA: 161.

Illustration Credits:
Bob Harvey, 11; Paul Dickinson, 26; Martin Cottam, 39; Paul Fisher
Johnson, 53-54; Thomas Sperling, 67, 69, 123, 125; Gerry Grace, 82;
Gillian McLean, 95-96; Nick Harris, 109, 111; Gwen Tourret, 153;
Peter Richardson, 165

*Copyright material on the following pages is reproduced by permission of Oxford
University Press:*
pp. 10–13 From Oxford Bookworms: The Withered Arm by Thomas Hardy
(retold by Jennifer Bassett) © Oxford University Press 2004; pp. 24–27
From Oxford Bookworms: The President's Murder by Jennifer Bassett ©
Oxford University Press 2000; pp. 38–41 From Oxford Bookworms: The
Phantom of the Opera by Jennifer Bassett © Oxford University Press 2000;
pp. 52–55 From Oxford Bookworms: The Adventures of Tom Sawyer by
Mark Twain (retold by Nick Bullard) © Oxford University Press 2000;
pp. 66–69 From Oxford Bookworms: Pocahontas retold by Tim Vicary
© Oxford University Press 2000; pp. 80–83 From Oxford Bookworms:
Christmas in Prague by Joyce Hannam © Oxford University Press 2000;
pp. 94–97 From Oxford Bookworms: The Wizard of Oz by L. Frank Baum
(retold by Rosemary Border) © Oxford University Press 2000; pp. 108–111
From Oxford Bookworms: The Elephant Man by Tim Vicary © Oxford
University Press 2000; pp. 122–125 From Oxford Bookworms: Aladdin and
the Enchanted Lamp retold by Judith Dean © Oxford University Press
2000; pp. 136–139 From Oxford Bookworms: The Coldest Place on Earth
by Tim Vicary © Oxford University Press 2000; pp. 150–153 From Oxford
Bookworms: A Little Princess by Frances Hodgson Burnett (retold by
Jennifer Bassett) © Oxford University Press 2000; pp. 164–167 From Oxford
Bookworms: Under the Moon by Rowena Akinyemi © Oxford University
Press 2000

*We would like to thank the following teachers, whose reviews, comments, and
suggestions contributed to the development of this series:*
Young-joo Bang, Myongji University, Korea; Pi-i Chuang, Chung Yuan
Christian University, Taiwan; Li-hui Chen, Tunghai University, Taiwan;
Larry Cisar, Kanto Gakuen Dai, Japan; Michelle Lee, Kaohsiung Hospitality
College, Taiwan; Stella Lee, Fooyin Universtiy, Taiwan; Shih-hao Lin,
Aletheia University, Taiwan; John Mancuso, Hitotsubashi University,
Japan; Michele Steele, Kyoai Gakuen, Takasaki Keizai, and Gunma Dai,
Japan; Chang-sup Sung, Dong-A University, Korea; Ki-wan Sung, Woosong
University, Korea; Hiroyo Yoshida, Toyo Daigaku Kogakubu, Japan.